Condos in the Woods

T0339931

WISCONSIN LAND AND LIFE

ARNOLD ALANEN
Series Editor

Spirits of Earth:
The Effigy Mound Landscape of Madison and the Four Lakes
ROBERT A. BIRMINGHAM

A Thousand Pieces of Paradise:
Landscape and Property in the Kickapoo Valley
LYNNE HEASLEY

Environmental Politics and the Creation of a Dream:
Establishing the Apostle Islands National Lakeshore
HAROLD C. JORDAHL JR., WITH ANNIE L. BOOTH

A Mind of Her Own: Helen Connor Laird and Family, 1888–1982
HELEN L. LAIRD

When Horses Pulled the Plow: Life of a Wisconsin Farm Boy, 1910–1929
OLAF F. LARSON

North Woods River: The St. Croix River in Upper Midwest History
EILEEN M. MCMAHON AND THEODORE J. KARAMANSKI

Buried Indians: Digging Up the Past in a Midwestern Town
LAURIE HOVELL McMILLIN

Wisconsin Land and Life: A Portrait of the State
EDITED BY ROBERT C. OSTERGREN AND THOMAS R. VALE

Condos in the Woods:
The Growth of Seasonal and Retirement Homes in Northern Wisconsin
REBECCA L. SCHEWE, DONALD R. FIELD, DEBORAH J. FROSCH,
GREGORY CLENDENNING, AND DANA JENSEN

Door County's Emerald Treasure: A History of Peninsula State Park
WILLIAM H. TISHLER

Condos in the Woods

The Growth of Seasonal and Retirement Homes in Northern Wisconsin

Rebecca L. Schewe, Donald R. Field, Deborah J. Frosch,
Gregory Clendenning, and Dana Jensen

THE UNIVERSITY OF WISCONSIN PRESS

The University of Wisconsin Press
1930 Monroe Street, 3rd Floor
Madison, Wisconsin 53711-2059
uwpress.wisc.edu

3 Henrietta Street
London WCE 8LU, England
eurospanbookstore.com

Copyright © 2012
The Board of Regents of the University of Wisconsin System
All rights reserved. No part of this publication may be reproduced, stored in a
retrieval system, or transmitted, in any format or by any means, digital, electronic,
mechanical, photocopying, recording, or otherwise, or conveyed via the Internet or
a website without written permission of the University of Wisconsin Press, except
in the case of brief quotations embedded in critical articles and reviews.

Printed in the United States of America

Library of Congress Cataloging-in-Publication Data
Condos in the woods: the growth of seasonal and retirement homes in northern
Wisconsin / Rebecca L. Schewe . . . [et al.].
p.   cm. — (Wisconsin land and life)
Includes bibliographical references and index.
ISBN 978-0-299-28534-0 (pbk.: alk. paper) — ISBN 978-0-299-28533-3 (e-book)
1. Burnett County (Wis.)—Social conditions. 2. Washburn County (Wis.)—
Social conditions. 3. Wisconsin—Rural conditions. 4. Vacation homes—
Wisconsin. 5. Second homes—Wisconsin. I. Schewe, Rebecca L.
II. Series: Wisconsin land and life.
F587.B95C66   2012
977.5'14—dc23
2011018263

Contents

Illustrations

TABLES

FIGURES

Acknowledgments

Thank you to our friends and colleagues for their support and advice during the preparation of this manuscript. Thank you especially to editor Steve Tomasko for his time and expertise. Thank you to our many reviewers and colleagues for your thoughtful comments and suggestions: Richard Krannich, A. E. Luloff, Thomas Rudell, Richelle Winkler, and our anonymous reviewers. Thank you to our partners and families for their patience and support and, most importantly, thank you the people and communities of northwestern Wisconsin for sharing their stories with us.

Condos in the Woods

Introduction

ALONG THE RURAL ROADS OF THE Wisconsin Northwoods around Sand Lake, the forested woodland occasionally breaks, revealing small cabins nestled in the trees and sometimes large, modern homes on the shoreline. On a summer evening most of the homes will be full of family and friends, lights in the windows and cars in the driveway. Visit between November and March, however, and many of the homes will be empty and cold, closed up for the season. In fact, fully one-half of the homes in the township of Sand Lake are vacant for much of the year because they are second homes, vacation homes for urban residents seeking recreation and relaxation in the Northwoods (Town of Sand Lake 2009). Sand Lake is not alone in this experience. Throughout the Northwoods and, in fact, throughout scenic rural communities around the nation and world, seasonal homeownership has expanded dramatically in recent decades as many communities have shifted toward recreation and tourism-based economies. These new communities have built their new economies and social structures on local natural amenities such as forests, waterways, and scenic vistas and are highly dependent on these non-extractive natural resources.

This transition has not always been painless as new residents move to communities and especially as the number of part-time residents has increased. Many rural residents and social scientists have found conflict and tensions in rural communities as residents struggle to create a new vision for their communities and to balance different priorities for the natural resources on which they depend. This is a story about the transformation of one such rural region—the Pine Barrens of northwestern Wisconsin and communities like Sand Lake. Although our story is set in one place, similar transformations are occurring in many areas of the United States as rural societies shift their focus, economies, and identities from one defined by extractive activities like forestry, mining, and agriculture into one defined by natural amenities such as scenic beauty, lakes, wildlife, and outdoor recreation. This is also a story about people. Along with, and perhaps because of, shifting relationships with natural amenities, the people moving to rural regions are changing. There are more seasonal residents and retirees, and there is a greater emphasis on service sector employment in rural communities. These changes in economy, community identity, and rural constituency have broad implications for local politics, land use planning, and the use of natural resources such as forests and lakes.

Throughout the communities at the heart of our story, we find reason for optimism about the current state and future of Sand Lake and other Northwoods communities. By understanding the integration of seasonal residents into their adopted Northwoods community, we have found that while there are important differences between seasonal and permanent residents, most shared a central vision for the future of their communities. These Northwoods communities are heavily dependent on their natural resources, and the common goals and environmental attitudes shared by diverse residents make us optimistic about the future as they move further into an era of non-extractive resource dependency.

In this book we offer a close examination of the people, a shifting rural lifestyle on the land, and the dynamic nature of change in rural communities. We describe the complex web of relationships between society and nature in a region where natural resources have been simultaneously extracted, developed, and protected, where the population is changing, and where work and play revolve around the aesthetic and recreational values and attributes of forests and lakes.

The ebbs and flows of rural population change in recent decades are directly and indirectly tied to changing relationships between communities and their natural resources. As traditional extractive industries (production landscapes) decline in importance, traditional land uses and those dependent upon them become a backdrop of "props on the rustic stage" (Pahl 1966, 307). For Halfacree and Boyle (1998), rural places became commodified for their amenities and aesthetics, thus their use of the term "post-productivist countryside." Similarly, Walker and Fortmann (2003) argue many rural areas struggled over the idea and imagery of landscape between those who support productive uses of the land and those who support aes-thetic and consumptive uses of the land. This ideology of landscape serves as a proxy for a number of conflicts within communities, including class conflict, cultural conflict, and struggles for control over local decision mak-ing. Simply said, this in-migration that has characterized the last several decades has brought newcomers who have had social, economic, and polit-ical impacts on their new rural communities.

A critical issue that emerged for many residents was the preservation of rural landscapes. Newcomers preferred to preserve their idealized land-scape of rolling hills, farms, forests, and open spaces (Halfacree and Boyle 1998; Halseth 1998; P. Nelson 2001; Shumway and Lethbridge 1998; Smutny 2002; Walker and Fortmann 2003). In contrast, many longtime residents supported growth and development, seeing growth as a means to provide jobs for themselves and their children (P. Nelson 2001; Spain 1993; Walker and Fortmann 2003). Similar differences were often reflected in the management priorities of neighboring public lands and forests. New residents, who often held negative views of extractive management policies, pushed for changes in public management priorities that favored preser-vation, the environment, and recreation (Egan and Luloff 2000; P. Nelson 2001; Rudzitis 1999).

Our research focuses on the following questions: How have rural com-munities been transformed when people more highly value a consumption landscape over a production landscape? How has the growth of seasonal residency reshaped the landscape of rural regions and communities rich in natural amenities? What does the future hold for amenity-rich rural communities with increasing numbers of newcomers and seasonal resi-dents? People have long been drawn to the natural beauty of Wisconsin's Northwoods, which has led to much amenity development and a high con-centration of seasonal homes—shifting the area's economy and natural re-sources from a production to a consumption landscape. This transition has brought fundamental changes in community structure, employment, and values toward natural resources for local communities. For many commu-nities the lumberyards have closed and logging operations have contracted, while the service sector has expanded and construction jobs increased. Internet cafes and gourmet coffee shops, along with cell towers, are becom-ing a common community fixture.

A key element of this book is the three-tier analysis we use to answer these research questions; we move from a national to regional to local focus.

We look closely at the people, the nature of change in rural communities, and a shifting rural lifestyle on the land by combining these three levels of analysis. First, we look at demographic trends of rural in-migration, housing development, and seasonal home ownership on a national scale, primarily using U.S. decennial census data. Then we narrow our perspective to examine trends in the Upper Midwest region, with particular emphasis on the Northwoods of Wisconsin. This national and regional examination defines the change from production to consumption landscapes in the north and sets the stage for our local-scale analysis of community change in Burnett and Washburn Counties—the Pine Barrens. The development of our key informant interviews, survey measures, and community analysis in this smaller study area was informed by the trends seen on national and regional scales.

While rural American communities have transformed significantly from production to consumption landscapes at the national level, northwestern Wisconsin has undergone its own changes. The region was once dominated by an extractive timber industry, but it is now a regional tourism and recreation destination because of the amenity values of its lakes and forests. Former logging towns now invite hunters, boaters, snowmobilers, and other visitors. Located just a two- to three-hour drive from Minneapolis and St. Paul, Burnett and Washburn Counties are an ideal location for seasonal residents from the surrounding urban areas. Burnett and Washburn are also covered with hundreds of gorgeous glacial lakes and rivers surrounded by regrowth forests. The remarkably high levels of seasonal residency in these two counties reflect the intersection of two major trends in second-home development: proximity to urban areas and high recreation potential. The story of our study area in the Wisconsin Pine Barrens parallels the stories of many amenity-rich rural communities.

Social scientists have expended considerable research energy to document population, housing, and employment change in amenity-rich counties throughout the United States and in doing so have learned a great deal about patterns of living in rural America. Census data primarily using counties as the unit of analysis has been the basis for much of this examination of new rural economies and communities (see Beale and Johnson 1998; Cromartie 1998; Frey and Johnson 1998; Frey and Speare 1992; Fuguitt 1985; Johnson and Beale 2002; McGranahan 1999; Rudzitis 1999). For example, exploring new American migration trends and the social values shaping them, McGranahan (1999) offered a unique explanation of a recent rebound in rural population. Through the quantification of desirable natural amenities, such as beautiful views, sunny climates, and the presence of forests, lakes, and mountains, McGranahan used county-level data to document the importance that natural amenities have in driving population change. He found that counties with high levels of natural amenities had higher levels of growth and in-migration than those without, showing the importance of the natural environment in shaping demographic change. In a complimentary analysis, Calvin Beale and Kenneth Johnson (1998) explored the role of human-made recreation amenities in new migration trends. Examining the presence of recreation infrastructure, such as amusement parks and other factors including tourism employment, Beale and Johnson (1998) found that nonmetropolitan counties with abundant recreational resources experienced more population growth and in-migration than those without.

Both of these analyses rely on the county as a unit of analysis and on large census data sets to tell the story of rural change. They demonstrate large trends in increasing population, seasonal housing growth, and the changing composition of rural economies and populations. It is important, however, for us to further develop the understanding of rural transformation by moving to a smaller scale and using different sources of data. Winkler and colleagues (2007) conducted one study that does this in examining rural community change in the western United States by considering a variety of indicators of amenity-driven rural change: seasonal home development, tourism employment, migration, and so on to represent the "New West." Then they classify communities on the municipal level, moving beyond the county to provide a more complex portrayal of where amenity-led development is occurring and to what extent.

We follow the example set by Winkler and colleagues (2007) both by moving beyond the county as the unit of analysis and by drawing upon unique survey data and key informant interviews to provide a more community-based understanding of rural transformation. We represent many of the same variables explored by Winkler and colleagues (2007) within our production/consumption landscape framework to illustrate the changing occupational and business structure when a community moves from an extractive production-based economy to a consumption-amenity based economy.

Our goal in this book is to illustrate the importance of human perception and identity of natural resources in driving rural community change and to explore the dynamics of new consumption landscapes. Rural space, in other words, is a combination of human behavior and the ecological parameters of the environment. The Pine Barrens of Wisconsin is one such rural space in which people have over time defined, redefined, and reshaped the environment on which they depend for their livelihoods. In short, the cultural imprint on the land is changing as retirees and seasonal residents become dominant players in the Pine Barrens. In doing so, we explore a range of data and sources to tell our story.

We are impressed with the strength, determination, and resiliency of communities in the Northwoods as they struggle to integrate the diversity of citizens moving to the country. We thank them for allowing us to share their rural space for a short time.

chapter 1

Rural People and the Land

THIS IS A STORY OF NORTHWESTERN WISCONSIN. A story about the transformation of a rural region once defined by the dominant extractive activities of forestry, mining, and agriculture into one defined by the non-extractive amenity attributes of the land, forests, lakes, and wildlife. It is also a story about people—the diversification of a rural region's population, the emergence of a new rural constituency (seasonal residents and retirees), and the expansion of a rural economy based on service sector employment. Finally, it is a story about the changing shape and culture of rural logging communities, their structure and function, as well as citizen relations, governance, and employment. Rapid population growth, coupled with huge increases in seasonal housing, new economic diversity, and changing population characteristics are altering the fundamental nature of some rural American communities in ways that have yet to be fully explored and understood. This is a story of the redefinition of nature and natural resource management in one natural amenity-rich region and the changing character of its rural communities—a story of change from an emphasis on extraction of natural resources to one of preservation of natural resources.

Many rural American communities like those in the Northwoods of Wisconsin now rely heavily on tourism, recreation, and second home-ownership rather than traditional extractive industries such as agriculture, mining, and forestry. Nevertheless, these communities remain heavily dependent on their natural resources. Local landscapes, waterways, forests, and scenic vistas are the lifeblood of these communities' identity and economy, and this heavy dependence on natural resources leaves communities potentially vulnerable to conflicting views of the environment and subject to the instability of nature. While this new non-extractive resource dependency may increase community vulnerability, in the story of these communities of northwestern Wisconsin we find reason for optimism in the shared vision and values of many diverse residents of the Northwoods.

Before moving ahead, we need to define some terminology we use throughout this book. Central to the book are the concepts of *production* and *consumption landscapes*. A production landscape is one in which the community places a high value on extracting natural resources from the land—timber, crops, and ores—and the primary employment is in forestry, agriculture, mining, and supportive services for those industries. A consumption landscape, however (and perhaps counter-intuitively), is a place where what is "consumed" is the landscape itself; people prioritize leaving the natural resource amenities in place because natural resources are valued for their aesthetic and recreation potential. In a consumption landscape, the community places more importance on features such as intact forests for hiking, clean water for boating, swimming, and fishing, scenic views and mountains for skiing, to name a few. Employment shifts in consumption landscape communities to support professional services, the real estate and financial sectors, construction, and tourism and recreation. We delve deeper into these terms later in this chapter. In this book we also use the broader term *cultural landscape* to illustrate the social meanings people place on nature. Cultural landscapes are the intersection of society and natural resources, referring to the different values and meanings that people give natural resources. Production and consumption landscapes are two different subcategories of cultural landscapes that reflect different social meanings of natural resources. We must also define our use of the term *amenity* or *amenity-rich* areas or landscapes. In this book, we use the term to mean *natural amenities* such as lakes, forests, and mountains, as we describe above for consumption landscapes.

We tell our story in the tradition of rural sociology, which emphasizes the relationship of people and the land as a basis for understanding rural life, social patterns, and communities. Communities socially define their natural resources, and therefore the natural environment is subject to transformation and redefinition (Greider and Garkovich 1994). In many rural regions with strong natural amenity attributes, this has meant that production landscapes once defined by agriculture, forestry, fisheries, or mining have been transformed into consumption landscapes defined by nature trails, parks, ski resorts, sport fishing, seasonal housing developments, and residential enclaves adjacent to public lands. This shift from production to consumption landscapes in natural amenity-based communities is related to social transformations of the communities; as the composition and self-definition of communities change, they redefine natural resources. These include the recomposition of the population to include more seasonal residents, retirees, and newcomers, new sources of employment and types of business enterprises, as well as changes in community organizations and resident participation in community affairs. New migrants and seasonal residents have helped to redefine the natural environment from a production landscape into a consumption landscape in which the aesthetic and recreation components of natural resources are consumed.

However, natural amenity-rich rural communities do not exist in isolation. Communities and residents are partners in a globalized world where multiple levels of complex interconnections need to be recognized. Our work includes a three-tier analysis in which we analyze national and regional trends as a context for understanding change in the local social and environmental landscape. We broadly examine the changes that rural communities are experiencing in terms of migration, new residents, and employment before we delve into what these changes could mean for communities. Are rural communities floundering under the pressures of development? Do new and old residents hold conflicting values and goals for their communities and natural resources? How do seasonal residents integrate into their host communities? And finally, how are communities once dependent on rural production landscapes adapting to new consumption landscapes? These are the community questions that drive our examination of the Wisconsin Northwoods.

We begin our story by sketching the historical pathway taken by European pioneers and settlers in northwest Wisconsin before we turn our attention to contemporary issues facing rural communities in the region. In particular, we focus on the rise of seasonal residents and their role in reshaping the social environment of a natural amenity-rich land and lakes region called the Pine Barrens of Wisconsin. Our research suggests that the migration of newcomers and seasonal residents to the Northwoods of Wisconsin may be somewhat unique from other high natural amenity regions. Unlike migrants to regions like the Intermountain West, many of these newcomers have previous ties or experiences with the land and lakes forming the Northwoods. Further, the conflicts between retirees, newcomers, seasonal residents and long-time residents noted elsewhere in the United States are somewhat muted in northwestern Wisconsin, suggesting more common ground on community and environmental issues.

PRODUCTION/CONSUMPTION LANDSCAPES AND
RESOURCE DEPENDENCY

The subject of rural communities and their ties between people and the land is a dominant thread in the literature of rural sociology (Field and Burch 1988). During the first half of the twentieth century, early attempts by rural sociologists to describe rural communities focused on the trade center and countryside population connection as a way to describe rural life, rural social relations, and community. Lowry Nelson's (1955) description of the rural community illustrates this focus: "[community is] that form of association maintained between the people and their institutions in a local area in which they live on dispersed farmsteads and in a village which usually forms the center of their common activity" (71). The ties between people and the land defined the character of a rural community, its structure, and its function.

Rural towns and villages developed a bond with the rural open-country population—the farmer, rancher, and forester. As a result, a symbiotic relationship existed between rural towns and adjacent rural landowners. Nelson further elaborates: "the trade center community is made up of two population components, the people of the trade center and the farm families in the area 'tributary' to the center" (L. Nelson 1955, 71). Businesses established in small rural trade centers depended on the support of rural residents living on the outskirts of town to keep their enterprise viable. Primitive means of transportation during the nineteenth century and at the beginning of the twentieth century made trade centers within close proximity to the rural landowner an indispensable component of country living. Kolb and Polson (1933) describe the importance of rural towns: "They are the major centers for merchandizing, banking and services for the countryside such as feed and seed stores, and grain mills as well as for the social and educational services of the community represented by high school, library, and other forms of recreation. In these services they serve the entire surrounding country areas" (28). There was, in other words, a reciprocal relationship between the trade center and the countryside population, a close bond in a production landscape.

Forestry Trade Centers

Settlement in rural forested communities led to similar relations between the trade center and the countryside; both agricultural and forestry communities related to their natural resources as a production landscape. Lumbering activities were the economic backbone of many towns and villages that formed during the time of early European settlement. A vast majority of the economic activities enjoyed by the townspeople were intrinsically tied to logging because they directly (or indirectly) involved loggers, lumber yards, logging equipment dealers, or the processing of timber at the local mills. As with early farming communities, the communities that arose in lumber areas supported local townspeople as well as those countryside people who surrounded the village. A symbiotic relationship developed between loggers and logging towns. The logging community is similar to the farming community in that large, unpopulated tracts of land are required for profitable resource extraction; therefore population density tended to be low: "Since the production region must be distant from the largest markets if it demands, as timber does, expanses of unpopulated lands, and since these activities are also specialized and require full-time institutional activity, these services are likely to be provided by urban centers" (Marchak 1983, 16).

In the United States, timber extraction gradually moved westward as timber supplies dwindled in the East. Logging towns emerged in much the same way that mining towns grew in relation to ore deposits—within close proximity to the resource (Gough 1997; Kates 2001; Landis 1997). In regions developed by early timber companies, the local trade center would support blacksmith shops, livery stables, saw mills, hotels, saloons, and other services related to timber extraction. Loggers who came to town to gather supplies and to socialize made up a large portion of the "countryside" population surrounding the early logging villages.

A single company often dominated small towns relying on resource extraction, and all other businesses and institutions within the community had intimate ties to this primary industry. The dominant company had great influence on the people who settled within the community and the surrounding area and the type of businesses supported within the community (Gates 1965). This often led to hardships that were difficult to resolve for the small rural community when the overall economy was slow. If no other thread ties the people of the village and the countryside population together, the community will decline if and when the dominant company pulls out. This phenomenon is especially prominent in relation to non-rnewable resources. In an effort to maximize profits, the goal of many lumber barons was to extract timber as quickly and efficiently as possible (Gates 1965; Kaufman and Kaufman 1946). Early timber companies would exploit forest resources and move on to the next forest (Kates 2001). Residents of these small logging towns were then left to fend for themselves to keep the economy and community going as the industry, along with many loggers, moved on.

Many small, rural communities suffered dire economic circumstances when the timber resources declined and agricultural pursuits failed. While this can be attributed to many influences, the primary reasons for the hardships experienced in these communities were twofold: an overdependence on resource extraction resulting in a lack of diversification of the economic structure and an incomplete institutional infrastructure necessary for community development, and inaccessibility to goods and services due to the remote location of these communities. Some communities managed to maintain a stable population by diversifying their economy and redefining their natural resources into a consumption landscape; some communities flourished, others simply vanished.

Resource Dependency

Rural communities and land use were often defined in terms of the strength and structure of the extractive economy—forestry, fishing, agriculture, and mining—in a specific region surrounding a community. Rural trade centers and country partners can be best understood as a "resource dependent community" existing within a production landscape. Theories of production and consumption landscapes go hand in hand with concepts of resource dependency.

The term *resource dependency* refers to the situation of isolated rural communities that rely heavily on extractive industries in the surrounding countryside. In this book, we define extractive resource dependency as the *production landscape* in which a community and its countryside population rely on agriculture or forestry for the majority of its economic activity. In northwestern Wisconsin, the extraction of timber has prevailed since the 1850s, and the structure of community—its social organization, employment, and business practices—mirrors the nature of the dominant extractive activity. This is the resource dependent *production landscape* historically prevalent in northwestern Wisconsin.

Economic measures are often used to define resource dependency and production landscapes (Beckley 1996; Force, Machlis, and Zhang 2000; Kaufman and Kaufman 1946; Machlis, Force, and Balice 1990; Peluso, Humphrey, and Fortmann 1994). Force, Machlis, and Zhang (2000) define resource dependent communities as "those with employment in specific resource industries far in excess of regional, state, and national levels" (411). Fortmann et al. (1991) use areas with 3 percent or higher wages in forest-related industries or with 50 percent or more of the land cover in timberland (see also Bliss, Walkingstick, and Bailey 1998) while Elo and Beale (1983) use 20 percent of total employment in the forest industry as an indicator of dependency. Salazar, Schallau, and Lee (1986) considered a county to have strong ties to the forest products industry if one third or more of its basic earnings were related to forest products. Additional indicators used by researchers to measure forest dependency may include population change, social institutions created primarily for those involved in resource-related activities, and resource production. Economic variables that are used to define resource dependency allow comparisons to be made regarding changes that occur within and between communities over time. Dependency in specific communities can then be compared to state and national trends as we do throughout this book.

Timber-dependent towns were those whose community and countryside population worked in some facet of the forest industry or in related support services. As with the analysis of agricultural trade centers, research on communities dependent on forestry for economic security was measured in terms of forestry employment and individual associated occupations (Haynes 2003). Small-town trade centers in timber areas depended on their ties to loggers and others in the countryside, and vice versa, in similar ways to the agricultural towns described by Lowry Nelson (1955) and the mining towns studied by Landis (1997).

Today the relationship between community and countryside is changing as the technology in extractive industries such as farming, forestry, and mining has improved operational efficiency. Technological change in these industries has resulted in fewer families and rural workers from these industries living on the land, supporting community businesses, participating in town or county governance, or providing an adequate school enrollment to maintain academic programs in schools or the schools themselves. These changes in extractive industries have helped set the stage for the redefinition of rural landscapes into consumption landscapes based on recreation and aesthetic values of natural resources. The link between people, the communities they create, the technology they employ, and the resources they exploit has transformed rural agriculture and forestry practices of yesterday and the landscapes they create.

Production and Consumption Landscapes Explored

To understand the link between rural communities and natural resources, it is useful to focus on rural cultural space. In *Understanding Ordinary Landscapes* editors Groth and Bressi (1997) provide a range of writers who discuss various aspects of cultural landscapes ranging from historical accounts to contemporary visions. Groth (1997) sets the tone by noting, "all human intervention with nature can be considered as cultural landscapes" (1). Greider and Garkovich (1994) offer a complimentary theory of the social construction of nature and landscape. The authors argue that landscapes are socially constructed and reconstructed. Natural resources are neither fixed nor physically defined; rather, "landscapes are the symbolic environments created by human acts of conferring meaning to nature and the environment" (1). The same natural resources—the trees of northwestern Wisconsin—can be socially constructed as "timber" within a production landscape and later redefined as "forests" within a consumption landscape. As communities change and redefine themselves they also redefine their natural landscapes and resources. The community can shape the countryside, and similarly the countryside can shape the community.

We connect these theories of cultural landscapes with earlier works of rural sociology concerned with the relationship between people and the land and the human patterns that result. Maher, Townsend, and Sanderson (1934) present one such historical study on production landscapes and change in those landscapes. This story of agricultural production of hops in New York State in the late 1800s illustrated the interplay of community structure, agricultural workforce, and a production landscape and examined what can happen if environmental factors change the conditions under which farming takes place in that landscape. Hops production, a dominant agricultural activity in New York State, relied on an hourly wage earner and migratory workers. A community support system of businesses and agricultural supply dealers evolved to cater to this form of agriculture. With constant production, however, soils became more acidic and yields declined. Eventually this agricultural industry became unfeasible, and in the end hop agriculture moved west, replaced by a different kind of production landscape—family-operated dairy farms and a different kind of cultural base for the community. The shift in agricultural production practices and workforce characteristics was accompanied by associated changes in the structure and function of community and the social institutions. Feed and seed businesses, grain elevators, and farm implement dealers emerged to support the people living there and the dairy farming industry (Maher, Townsend, and Sanderson 1934). The ties, however, between land, work, and community continued, and the signposts for a new production landscape arose.

In the classic case study *Three Iron Mining Towns*, Landis (1997, originally published in 1931) compares the social and cultural changes that have taken place in three mining towns in the Mesabi Range of Minnesota as they shifted from dependence on forests and forestry to developing their iron ore industry. While Landis does not use the term *cultural landscape*, he meticulously traces the changes the towns experienced in population, politics, social relations, institutions, and culture, building fundamentally upon new definitions of the natural resources in the area. He builds a theory of cyclical change in which there is a causal relationship between physiosocial cycles, biosocial cycles, psychosocial cycles, and cultural cycles. As iron was discovered, boomed, and then declined, so did the social networks and community institutions of Virginia, Hibbing, and Eveleth. The social fabric of the towns was inextricably bound to their natural environment, and as the environment was transformed by human activity the human community and associated institutions were transformed. These two classic stories of hops production in upstate New York (Maher, Townsend, and Sanderson 1934) and the mining country of Minnesota (Landis 1997) illustrate the historical ebb and flow of people and communities and how cultural landscapes, in these cases production landscapes, evolve and change.

Today we are looking at another rural landscape, one not defined by agriculture or forestry production but rather by the aesthetic qualities of the land, lakes, forests, and mountains. These landscapes are also cultural landscapes but of a different type. They can be described by their modern structures: hotel chains, gourmet coffee shops, Internet cafes, ski resorts, lake associations, and condominiums. These landscapes are *consumption landscapes* built upon the natural amenity assets in the region. In northwestern Wisconsin, the town of Siren illustrates the change from production to consumption landscapes. Siren was once a forestry town, but its central business district was devastated by a tornado in summer 2001. The town leaders, with the support of citizens and the business community, crafted a strategy to reconstruct Main Street in a log cabin motif. Now there are modern hotel complexes, Internet cafes, and market centers. The cultural landscape here suggests a community image and identity of recreation and tourism—that is, a consumption landscape. Throughout this book we illustrate the shift in these cultural landscapes from production to consumption landscapes in natural amenity regions through the eyes of local communities and the residents living there and in the countryside, both seasonal and permanent.

A Further Note on Consumption Landscapes

We continue to think that a rural community can be characterized by the composition of the population living within the community and in the countryside and their relationship to their natural resources. At one time, employment sources in the local area and the residential population density of the immediate region defined resource dependency. Today, however, such factors are insufficient to describe a community's ties to natural resources and the residents in surrounding landscapes. We agree with Winkler and colleagues (2007), who, in their examination of community structure in the Intermountain West, suggest that communities located in natural amenity landscapes differ from their more traditional counterparts in significant ways. Communities with natural amenity attributes have greater employment diversity, especially in the service sector, professions, and construction industries, more retirees, higher rates and numbers of housing construction, higher housing values, higher personal income, and declining employment in extractive industries. Nevertheless, dependency on the natural resource continues even in a consumption landscape. This is especially evident in ski resort communities, where the fluctuation in snowfall and snow accumulation throughout the season can influence the ebb and flow of tourism travel. The same could be said for gateway communities on the borders of public lands such as national parks, where visitation corresponds to the seasons of the year, school schedules, and weather. Like other resource-dependent communities, consumption landscapes are also subject to the whims of nature and the resulting patterns of human-nature relations.

We suggest that a new type of resource dependency in natural amenity regions arises when rural communities and their neighboring populations develop a mutually supporting social and economic structure designed to capture the non-extractive attributes of mountains, forests, lakes, rivers, and public lands. *Non-extractive resource dependency* is the consumption of nature and natural resources of the area for their aesthetic and recreational value. The structure of community and its social organization, employment, and business practices mirror the character of the dominant natural amenity attributes captured by community. This is the case for many communities in the Wisconsin Northwoods.

TRANSFORMATION OF THE NORTHWOODS TO A CONSUMPTION LANDSCAPE

We describe the dynamic nature of people, the land, and the changing patterns of the rural Northwoods as the region transforms from a production landscape represented by forest extraction and the accompanying community structure to a consumption landscape represented by communities that are capturing the aesthetic attributes of nature and the land. We illustrate the transformation of these landscapes by drawing upon the critical variables noted by Winkler and her colleagues (2007) when describing communities in the Intermountain West that are transforming themselves from Old West (traditional extractive communities) to New West communities that have adopted recreation and tourism development.

Traditional forest extractive resource communities of the Northwoods revolved around the logging and milling technology employed in the industry, the transportation system available for shipping logs to market, and the business enterprises serving local families and the forest industry (see figure 1.1). Much of the early logging occurred in the winter, and shipping of logs relied on the river system (Gates 1965; Kates 2001; Rohe 1984). River transport was subsequently replaced by railroads, which were later supplemented and largely supplanted by road systems and logging trucks (Kates 2001). Larger tracts of land in remote regions were opened as transportation improved and the technology of timber harvesting advanced. Consequently fewer small logging communities were needed to support the industry. As with the transformation in agriculture—from horse to tractor to massive GPS-equipped combines—forestry as an industry has continually evolved, including the adoption of robotics in many milling practices. In both cases, changes in technology and transportation impacted the employment base, requiring fewer workers in the industry and fewer residents to participate in community affairs. As a result, numerous rural communities dependent on farming and forestry declined or disappeared completely.

Replacing the traditional extractive forestry community is a contemporary set of relationships spawned by a new migration to rural places and new types of consumption of natural resources. New migrants are not dependent on the forest industry but rather choose to reside in the natural amenity-rich forested countryside. Contemporary migration to nonmetropolitan areas for quality-of-life factors and natural amenities was first described in the nonmetropolitan turnaround of the 1970s (Fuguitt 1985). Marans and Wellman (1978) documented the importance of natural amenity migration to rural midwestern communities and the social conflict that can arise from this new migration. David McGranahan's report (1999), *Natural Amenities Drive Rural Population Change*, helped to quantify this recent pattern of rural migration. In this study, McGranahan develops a natural amenity index that quantifies each county's level of desirable natural amenities such as diverse topography, water coverage, and climate. He then examines the migration in and out of counties using a variety of control variables (poverty, county economic type, and urbanity) along with his natural amenity index. His results demonstrate the importance of natural amenities in predicting recent

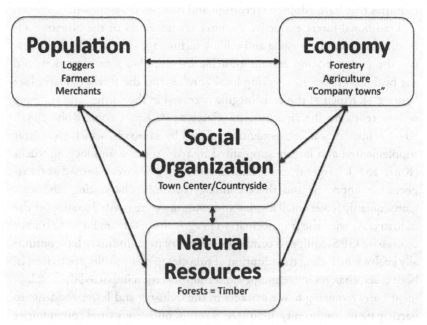

FIGURE 1.1. Elements of a production landscape

migration. Similarly, Johnson and Beale (2002) found that nonmetropolitan counties classified as recreation counties (high-wage and salary employment in entertainment and recreation, accommodations, eating and drinking places, and real estate as a large percentage of all employment, and high seasonal housing concentration) demonstrated about twice as much population growth during the decade 1990–2000 as other nonmetropolitan counties. Thus, Johnson and Beale's work also confirms the increasing importance of recreation and aesthetics in driving recent rural migration patterns.

Figure 1.2 depicts this twenty-first-century connection between population and community in high natural amenity environments with a second view of our rural landscape where employment in the service sector, seasonal housing ownership, and number of homes constructed have flourished. Internet cafes, regional medical centers, hotel chains, specialty shops, and large multifunction marketplaces have replaced the corner grocery stores, local pharmacy, and family-owned motel. This is the emerging consumption landscape for many rural places in Wisconsin Northwoods communities and the communities in the Pine Barrens of Wisconsin.

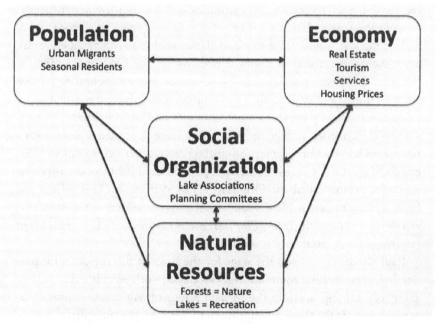

FIGURE 1.2. Elements of a consumption landscape

The following chapters of the book trace the historical transformation of Wisconsin Northwoods communities from production to consumption landscapes. In chapters 1 through 4 we document this transformation and illustrate that a consumption landscape overlays the social environment of the Northwoods communities. In chapters 5 through 8 we explore the social reality of this consumption landscape.

THE NORTHWOODS OF WISCONSIN:
A UNIQUE NATURAL AMENITY SETTING

Most locals think of the Northwoods of Wisconsin as those counties spanning the upper reaches of the state north of Highway 8, from the Minnesota border to Lake Michigan. From a tourism perspective, however, northern Wisconsin can be divided into three subregions: the eastern border and Door County, the central Northwoods counties, and the western border counties. Each subregion of the north has its own resident and tourist profile. The eastern border and Door County form a travel corridor to the north dominated by residents of Illinois; the central Northwoods counties attract predominately Wisconsin and Illinois residents (Stedman 2006); and the western border counties draw a high number of Minnesota residents seeking outdoor recreation opportunities and vacation homes in northwestern Wisconsin. Extensive studies by Stedman (2000, 2002, 2003, 2006, and 2008) and others (Gobster and Rickenbach 2004; Schnaiberg et al. 2002; Schroeder 2002) of seasonal homeowners and recent migrants in the central to eastern areas of the Northwoods provide grounding for our study of northwest Wisconsin. The common ecological and regional social character shared by northeastern Minnesota and northwestern Wisconsin reflects a historic timber and mining resource dependency along with a recreation and tourism connection distinct from other subregions of Wisconsin. Our story is set in the western portion the Northwoods, a specific ecological region called the Pine Barrens of Wisconsin. Throughout the book we use the term *Northwoods* to refer to the larger region of northern Wisconsin and the terms *Pine Barrens* or *northwestern Wisconsin* when referring to our specific study area.

Paul Landis (1997) sets the stage for the story of this region in his pioneering work on rural communities. His classic work on cultural change in three iron-mining towns in the Mesabi Range of Minnesota continues to serve as a guide for those attempting to understand the interplay of people and the land. The opening description of his study area places resource dependency and the evolution of community and rural society into context. He notes:

> Driving northward in Minnesota some two hundred miles above the Twin Cities, one reaches a wilderness of burned-over stumps, second-growth ever-greens, tamarack, and underbrush scattered over rocky hills intervened by swampy valleys or crystal lakes. An occasional farmhouse suggests the presence of human life. The area bespeaks an age of timber now past some thirty years, and agriculture as yet unborn. The charred stumps and deadened trees indicate the passing of devastating fires. The highway at a distance of some sixty miles north of Duluth leads into cities located in the most unsuspected places—cities blotted on the rugged surface features of an iron range. (3)

Driving a similar distance from the Twin Cities along Wisconsin's western border, travelers find themselves in the landscape called the northwestern Pine Barrens of Wisconsin. Although the Pine Barrens is only a portion of what many Wisconsinites call the Northwoods, this natural area boasting numerous lakes and forests one hundred miles south and east of the Mesabi Iron range is a vital part of the mythic Northwoods.

We conducted research in this rural region of northwestern Wisconsin. The Pine Barrens region, whose origin can be traced back to the end of the last glaciations, is a land mass defined by distinct physical characteristics, specifically the geology, soil, water regimes, and habitat type (Northwest 2000; Radeloff et al. 1998). The remnants of a retreating glacier character-ized by sandy, nutrient-limited soils, the Pine Barrens is a patchwork of pine forests, hardwoods, lakes, large outwash plains, and open prairie. The physical region of 1,500 square miles spans the administrative boundaries of five counties in northwestern Wisconsin: Bayfield, Douglas, Burnett, Wash-burn, and Polk.

This region supports an abundance of wildlife: whitetail deer abound in large numbers; a diversity of migratory bird species frequent the region; the native wild lupine plants support the endangered Karner blue butterfly; timber wolf packs have reclaimed some of their native territory. The Wis-consin Department of Natural Resources participates in a program to re-introduce elk in the northern forested landscape, and a small number of moose meander back and forth across the region.

The region is also a mosaic of public and private land ownership. Human settlement has expanded throughout the region, particularly in forested areas, along lakes, and adjacent to public lands. We examine many aspects of change in all five Pine Barren counties. According to Wisconsin's *State Comprehensive Outdoor Recreation Plan* (SCORP), population in three of the five northwestern Wisconsin counties grew at twice the state average during the 1990s (*SCORP* 2005). Because of the popularity of the region for second-home development, growth is more accurately measured by increases in both population and housing. The number of housing units is perhaps even more important in terms of impact on the landscape, increasing nearly 50 percent between 1970 and 1990 (*SCORP* 2005).

To illustrate the growth of seasonal housing and seasonal residency we examine in depth the portion of this unique northwestern Wisconsin forest and lakes region located within Burnett and Washburn Counties. Situated just two to three hours from Minneapolis and St. Paul, Burnett and Washburn are an ideal location for urban seasonal residents. The region's long history of cottages reflects such patterns of growth. Burnett and Washburn are also covered with hundreds of gorgeous glacial lakes and rivers surrounded by second- and third-generation forests. The remarkably high levels of seasonal homeownership in these counties reflect the intersection of two major trends in second-home development: proximity to urban areas and high recreation or amenity potential (Coppock 1977c; Dower 1977; Ragatz 1970). Its population is also growing as retirees and telecommuters—those who can work remotely—find the rural ambience appealing. This growth is largely attributable to new people moving to the area as both counties experienced negative rates of natural increase, births minus deaths, during the 1990s (*SCORP* 2005).

Chapter Outlines

We apply the concepts of production and consumption landscapes to understand the complex web of relationships between society and nature in a region where natural resources have been simultaneously extracted, developed, and protected. The book also provides an in-depth look at a rural natural amenity region being transformed by new migrants to rural places. The signature element of this book is its three-tier analysis matching national and regional data with community and survey data offering a close examination of the people, the nature of change in rural communities, and a shifting rural lifestyle on the land. We begin in chapter 2 with a historical sketch of the different periods of transition in human settlement of the Pine Barrens to set the stage for our contemporary look at patterns on the land, the dynamic nature of people, and places in the natural amenity region called the Pine Barrens.

The Shift from Production to Consumption Landscapes

Chapter 3 introduces the larger context of the study by examining shifts from production to consumption landscapes and changes in population, housing, and economic conditions in rural areas on a national scale. We place the Wisconsin Northwoods within the national context of natural amenity-driven migration, housing, and community change. Rural communities across America are experiencing rapid and unprecedented social and demographic change. Few rural communities today maintain their traditional dependence upon extraction-based industries; instead they exhibit a variety of different development trajectories. For natural amenity-rich rural areas, one of the most prevalent development paths has been a shift toward tourism and recreation-based economies founded upon the abundance of local natural resources (Beale and Johnson 1998; Halfacree and Boyle 1998; Shumway and Otterstrom 2001; Smutny 2002). Patterns of exurbanization and expanding urban fringe development are also reshaping the rural/urban interface and are continuing to alter the nature of rural America (Audirac 1999; Fishman 1990; Lewis 1995; A. Nelson and Dueker 1990).

The Pine Barrens in a Regional Context

After we introduce the broader context for the study, the following chapters delve deeply into this Pine Barrens region, exploring the unique realities within this particular landscape. Chapter 4 traces the contemporary demographic history of the Pine Barrens, reflecting on how the changes experienced by Northwoods communities coincide with the larger migration, housing, and economic shifts of natural amenity-rich rural areas. Each community in the Pine Barrens has a unique social organization, community style, and personality, although common characteristics can be found among many. This chapter introduces the demographic and economic traits of the region and communities, highlighting common experiences. It also presents a more comprehensive view of the unique lifestyle and community features associated with the consumption landscape of the region. Seasonal residency, particularly of urbanites from the Twin Cities of Minnesota, is an important feature of the housing market and communities of the Pine Barrens. The role of seasonal residents in their host community is unclear and dynamic, with part-timers existing in a "grey world" somewhere

between tourists and full-time community members. Chapters 5 and 6 examine the social impacts of seasonal residency, exploring the social dynamics generated by the new patterns of natural amenity-led development and
implications for the social organization of community. These chapters consider how seasonal-home development has reshaped the social webs and
rural space of northwestern Wisconsin communities. In chapter 5, we
specifically examine the attachment of residents, both permanent and seasonal, to the natural environment and communities of the Northwoods.
Chapter 6 focuses on the participation of residents in community life and
the web of social ties. Together, these chapters analyze the new social
organization of the Northwoods that has accompanied the creation of a
consumption landscape. As communities have turned toward recreation
and tourism dependency, seasonal residency has become increasingly common. Seasonal residency has, in turn, reshaped the social webs of the communities, changing interpersonal relationships and community dynamics.

Human Behavior, Natural Resources, and Environment

Chapter 7 further explores the complicated incorporation of seasonal residents into the Northwoods' consumption landscapes by examining residents' attitudes toward natural resource management and planning. The
recreation-led development of rural America is dependent upon the natural
resources of a given area, frequently building upon a fragile ecosystem. The
environmental dangers of overuse and pollution are prominent concerns
for recreation communities whose entire livelihood and identity hinges on
the protection of natural resources. Resource management, then, is one of
the most important community issues in the Northwoods and, not surprisingly, one of the most contentious. Problematically, the resource management priorities and desires of seasonal residents often diverge significantly
from those of permanent rural residents (Gartner 1987; Girard and Gartner 1993; Green et al. 1996; Halseth 1998; Marans and Wellman 1978).
Chapter 7 explores resident attitudes toward public land management priorities, perceptions of community change, growth management, and private
property rights in a consumption landscape.

After telling the story of the Pine Barrens of Wisconsin, chapter 8 draws
attention to lessons learned from the case study to further our understanding of communities that are transitioning from production landscapes
to non-extractive consumption landscapes. What can we learn from our
study about natural amenity-rich rural America? What are the demographic

and social indicators of a community embracing natural amenity attributes? What does the future hold for rural communities that have created consumption landscapes? The options for environmental regulation and natural resource development are diverse, as are the social and cultural avenues for change. This final chapter summarizes our major findings, concludes with an overview and discussion of contemporary human–nature relations, and explores conservation issues community scholars should consider as they attempt to understand changing rural natural amenity landscapes in the twenty-first century.

chapter 2

The Pathway to Change and Settlement in the Pine Barrens

THIS STORY FEATURES THE TWENTY-FIRST-CENTURY cultural landscape and the current forces of change altering the social fabric of communities in the Pine Barrens of Wisconsin. But in order to understand the present transformation of the region, we briefly characterize the past human imprint on the land. To do this, we highlight the story of three communities, two of which were able to shift from their production landscape and build a consumption landscape on the natural amenity assets in the surrounding countryside.

The historical eras of northern Wisconsin Pine Barrens in many ways mirror changes faced by rural communities across America. Northern Wisconsin has evolved over time as the population and landscape changed. European settlement began with a *pioneering period* that ushered in the early arrival of lumber barons and lumbermen from around 1830 to 1889. This was a time when the production landscape of the Pine Barrens was established. A *settlement period* followed, marked by a surge in the arrival of European settler families to the frontier, a time when many of the northern communities were taking on a personality of their own and agriculture was heavily promoted. The period ended after the logging boom and many agricultural pursuits proved unsuccessful, around 1919. The *meandering period* occurred from 1920 through the 1940s when general population and economic decline for much of the region occurred (Gough 1997). But new economic revitalization took place in the region after the 1950s. The fourth era, from the 1960s to the present, the *rediscovery period*, marks a time when population again began to increase and tourism became an economic mainstay for many communities and people living in the region. A consumption landscape began to emerge.

THE PIONEERING PERIOD

As timber supplies in the eastern United States were exhausted, lumber companies found their way to the forests of northern Wisconsin. To assess the timber potential of the area, logging companies first sent in timber cruisers to determine the size of the area to be logged and the amount of timber present so that appropriate numbers of men and equipment could be dispatched. Thus began the pioneer period. Next came the men to build roads and camps, a supply division that brought in the equipment necessary to support men and animals, and finally the workers and equipment needed to do the logging (Marple 1979).

Timber harvesting occurred on a small scale in northern Wisconsin until the 1850s but soon became the backbone of the region's economy (Marple 1979). Logging activities were the primary incentive for those Europeans pioneering in the region because the forests provided a means for new settlers to earn a living. The earliest pioneer communities in the area were camps established to accommodate the multitude of lumberjacks who came from the East to seek employment. Camps were usually built within one mile of the logging activity—the distance a man could comfortably walk in one day and still put in a good day's work. These temporary establishments were easily uprooted and moved near the next great stand of trees to fell (Marple 1979).

Prior to the 1860s, logging camps were small and primitive. A crew of twelve to fifteen men typically needed only one building to provide sleeping, eating, and cooking quarters. The men slept in rough, wooden bunks or on the floor of the shack, which was heated with a small open fire. Eventually most camps would include a stable for horses or oxen and an equipment shed (Marple 1979). Much of community life in the Northwoods revolved around logging activity in this early era of resource dependency.

Before railroads made their way to this still-remote section of the world, water was the primary mode of transportation for cut timber. Companies built many dams on the region's small rivers and streams to aid in transportation of the logs. Water volume was strictly controlled on these waterways in an effort to direct the flow of timber. A dam operator cleared the stream of obstructions such as trees and boulders, sometimes with the aid of explosives. In some instances, canals shortened the course or bypassed dangerous stretches of river (Marple 1979). During the early years, the timber industry extracted only pine logs (or soft wood) because they floated well on the waterways. "White Pine had special characteristics: it floated, was of great length and diameter, was lightweight yet strong, and was easy to use in carpentry work" (Vogeler 1986, 95). Harder wood, such as oak, was prone to sinking in the water, thus making its harvest impractical until companies developed other means of transportation (Marple 1979).

Out of necessity, most logging was done in the winter. Loggers found it much easier to transport the massive pine logs across frozen rivers and marshes than to create and maintain roads throughout the year. Sparse and primitive roads made transportation slow and arduous, but basic *tote roads* were necessary to allow the movement of logs from the cutting site to the waterways. Often the roads were coated with ice to ease the movement of large shipments of timber (Marple 1979). Great piles of harvested timber were stored over the winter season, and the spring thaw would arrive with a roaring crack. Logs smashed their way downriver to the sawmills where workers would cut them into lumber. They tied the rough-cut boards together into rafts and floated them to wholesale markets in Chicago and also to cities along the Mississippi River (Davis 1997).

THE SETTLEMENT PERIOD

As logging activity increased, logging camps grew in number and size. By the 1880s more than one hundred loggers would often occupy a single logging camp. In turn, community facilities to support the logging activity became more sophisticated. Camps enlarged their stables to shelter more horses, oxen, sleds, and other road equipment. Crewmembers could secure clothing, tobacco, and other personal items from wannigans—small company stores located in camp. More permanent camps also included a blacksmith shop, carpentry and sharpening shops, a granary, hay sheds, a supervisor's quarters, separate mess halls, and bigger equipment sheds (Marple 1979). The seeds of a Northwoods community began to emerge, following the patterns of the trade center/countryside development.

The population and characteristics of the settlers shaped the social fabric of early communities. Those who forged the frontier were diverse: "The daring, the adventuresome, the lonesome lumberjack, the seasonal immigrant who at first returned annually to his homeland in Europe with his savings, the gambler, the outcast who wanted to hide from society, the prostitute, as well as the respectable and the elite" (Landis 1997, 18). Because of their resource dependency and the dominance of the lumber industry, communities were predominately male: "[Early] towns originally drew the male sex, many of them young adventuresome men without worldly possessions. . . .

Women came later, when the communities bade fair to be suitable for women" (19). According to historical accounts, loggers in northern Wisconsin were no exception to this pattern of "rough" development, and there was no shortage of saloons during the early logging period. But as camps grew in size and services, new business opportunities presented themselves, and women and children became more prominent as the lumber camps grew into more established communities. The Northwoods production landscape began to support more diverse resource-dependent communities.

In the late 1800s, agricultural development began in the Northwoods alongside the forestry industry. The Homestead Act of 1862 enabled new settlers to make land claims when the land in northern Wisconsin opened to homesteading in the early 1890s (Bawden 1997; Gates 1965; Kates 2001). By this time the lumber companies and land speculators had made claims on most of the prime land, and settlers had to accept what remained, which was often land with poor soil in more remote locations (Marple 1979). As agriculture spread, immigrants from many European countries came to join local communities and again altered the population and social fabric of the Northwoods.

Through the 1910s, however, lumbering activities were still the economic backbone of most towns and villages formed during the time of early settlement. The vast majority of the economic activities enjoyed by the townspeople were intrinsically tied to logging because they directly or indirectly involved loggers, logging equipment providers, associated logging companies, and mill operators. Communities expanded during this time to support local workers living within and outside the village. Following the pattern of trade center/countryside interdependence described by Nelson (1955), logging communities consisted of large, unpopulated tracts of land supporting small trade center towns.

A Tale of Three Towns

Many Northwoods settlements that depended on local logging activities met with hard times when the prime timber supplies were exhausted by the early 1900s. As in many early American settlements, logging in northern Wisconsin eventually gave way to the promotion of agriculture as "the plow followed the ax." Some towns, however, were less than successful in making this transition. A variety of factors caused such failure, many tied to the natural resources and amenities of the region. A unique soil type designates the Pine Barrens region of northwestern Wisconsin. The low-quality sandy soil found in the region is not conducive to large-scale agriculture. Climatic conditions and a short growing season were also a limitation faced by aspiring farmers. In addition, many small settlements were located in remote regions that were difficult to access with the primitive roads and methods of transportation. Some of the original towns developed in northern Wisconsin during the pioneer period were destined to be of a temporary nature.

One example of a vanished or "temporary" town is Veazie, once located in the heart of Washburn County. Veazie, like many early communities, started out as a "stopping place" along the route between larger settlements, and it grew as a result of its location close to a timber supply. Timber extraction was the base of economic activity and accounted for the majority of the commerce within the community and the people in the surrounding countryside.

Veazie Township

The growth of the timber industry and the arrival of the railroads brought many new settlers to the Pine Barrens area during the early 1880s. The rapid influx of people prompted the state legislature to split the previously established Burnett County into two separate political entities, thus establishing Washburn County. A dam was built in 1878 across the Namekogan River to aid in transportation of logs felled in the vicinity. The only settlement in the northern township during this time was near the Veazie logging dam. (A second settlement in Washburn County at the time was Bashan, located in the southern half of the county.) Officially christened in November 1880, Veazie settlement soon became a small lumbering community. Supplies for this newly established town were procured from Stillwater, Minnesota, via the Veazie Trail, an old logging tote road that ran along portions of northwestern Wisconsin.

After the railroad came to Veazie in 1881, the town grew quickly on both sides of the tracks. Original structures included horse and ox barns, a huge supply warehouse, and the famous Veazie House, a hotel established to accommodate supervisory personnel, lumberjacks, and travelers. This small logging community housed the headquarters of Walker, Judd, and Veazie, one of the biggest logging companies in northern Wisconsin during this period. It wasn't long before more organizational establishments made their way to town. Veazie soon boasted a town hall, a post office, a school, and a jail. The O'Brien brothers (John, James, and Edward), bought out Walker,

Judd, and Veazie in 1884 and continued the logging trade. Agnes Kennedy (1873–1958) was a member of the town of Veazie. She recounted her stories to Ward Winton, a historian from the area:

> Veazie Settlement . . . was the center of social life for the whole northern half of Washburn County. Here in the saloon of the old Veazie House the lumberjacks congregated, smoked, drank, told stories, and held dances. Here the early settlers from miles around came for their supplies, and to drink and dance and exchange news. Here was the center of all activities . . . life itself at Veazie was interesting with lumberjacks and other itinerants coming and going, the big logging teams coming in for supplies, the settlers coming in for their mail, the settlers and the loggers from the whole area coming in to vote on election days, and the huge log drives coming down the river and through the dam each spring. (Winton 1980, 129)

Veazie continued to grow for several years, with the core of the economy largely dependent on the logging industry. Many of the businesses in town supplied goods and services to the timber workers in the surrounding area. A huge warehouse housed logging supplies and equipment; two large log barns held horses and oxen. A blacksmith shop supplied shoes for horses and oxen and took care of the ironwork necessary for the logging camps. The town hall, schoolhouse, and post office were in one building while a saloon and jail were together in another (Winton 1980). While the existence of these community services indicates the town was growing in institutional structure, limited space was appropriated to these types of activities. This suggests that priority was given to businesses supporting the logging industry and that the particular community services were only necessary on a limited basis since there were few families with children in the area.

It would have been difficult to predict the downfall of Veazie during the boom period of logging activity. By the end of the 1890s, however, most of the red and white pine had been cut from the region. In 1898, the local lumber company sold all of its holdings in the town and severed the backbone of the community. Loggers living in the countryside left for better prospects elsewhere. The town, which had been so dependent on the logging business and the countryside people involved in logging, could no longer support itself. Shortly thereafter a fire burned out all of the buildings in the settlement. Ward Winton recounts:

Veazie Settlement disappeared with the end of the white Pine logging era around 1900. The Veazie dam went out [around] 1902. Where once was Washburn County's earliest settlement, the thriving, boisterous, logging community of Veazie, there is nothing now but a farmer's field, with even the basement of the old Veazie House no longer discernable, and only the earth abutments of the old logging dam, and the barely discernible logging road leading to it, to mark its existence. (Winton 1980, 130)

In 1904, the area once known as Veazie Township was renamed Spring Brook. Once the logging industry on which Veazie depended was gone, the remaining population did not generate enough commerce to support the community. When logging ended, few employment alternatives existed to replace employment in the timber industry. The lack of job opportunities gave the people in the community and adjacent region little choice but to relo-cate. The interdependent relationship between the community and the countryside people vanished. The emergence of new settlements nearby that could out-compete this remote settlement for trade also led to the demise of Veazie.

Iron River

Of course, not all towns established on the heels of logging suffered the same fate as Veazie. Located in the west central part of Bayfield County, Iron River also emerged in direct relation to the local timber industry and the quality timber stands within close proximity to the settlement (Lund 1975). The Bayfield Peninsula, located just northwest of Iron River, con-tained dense stands of large red and white pines. Access to the settlement was easy as many people traveled on the nearby St. Croix Trail, and Iron River lay conveniently along the Northwest Pacific Railroad route between the Wisconsin cities of Ashland and Superior.

Iron River was among the most prominent logging communities to emerge during the height of the logging era. Early on, Iron River Camp was just a sidetrack along the Iron River where men working to construct the Northern Pacific Railroad between Ashland, Wisconsin, and Duluth, Minnesota, set up camp. Frank Lore and his family are considered to be the first European residents of the settlement at Iron River, arriving around 1885. At the time, the railroad owned much of the land through govern-ment land grants.

Settler John Pettingill visited the area in the fall of 1887 as a deer hunter. He returned in spring of 1888 to establish a trading post and a land claim

after learning that homesteading was going to open the area to more settlement. By fall of the same year, he added a store, hotel, and post office
to accommodate the rapidly growing population. Even more European
settlers arrived after the land was opened to homesteading in 1890–1891
(M. Daniels 1992). The township included land a distance of forty miles by
eighteen miles. Because good land claims had a wealth of valuable pine timber, land was in high demand; the land claims office in Ashland had a line
of people four blocks long waiting to make claims in the Iron River vicinity.
During this boom period, lots sold quickly and buildings downtown went
up just as fast (Pettingill 1992). Most of the present business district of Iron
River is still located on Pettingill's original homestead claim (Savage 1992).

Iron River entrepreneurs anticipated the arrival of lumberjacks and
settlers. The first businesses in town were a trading post, sawmill, and
the Pettingill Lodge, a hotel that could accommodate up to 150 overnight
guests. In 1892, the population was estimated to be somewhere between
1,240 and 2,000 (*Iron River, Wisconsin Centennial* 1992). At the peak of the
lumbering activity, circa 1900, the population of Iron River was 2,439 (U.S.
Census 1900). The city boasted several general stores, twenty-two saloons,
one church (Presbyterian), a schoolhouse (estimated to cost $3,500), and
five lumber mills. The town business district was largely dependent on the
lumber mills (*Iron River Times* 1992). In addition, there were approximately
thirty lumber camps, thirty-seven saloons, and more than four thousand
lumberjacks living within a thirty-mile radius of the main business district
(Lund 1975).

Iron River is no exception to the rowdy settlement pattern described by
Landis (1997). In reference to Iron River, historian Fred P. Lund states:
"The people seem to take pleasure in referring to their town as the wild-
est, roughest and toughest of the timber country. . . . [Iron River] was a rip
snorter and she ran wide open and fast like the [fires] of hell. The drunks,
the fights, the killings, the gambling, and the loose women of the bawdy
houses were accepted as part of the times" (1975, 76).

Fires were common in the Pine Barrens region during this period, in part
because of the large amount of slash left behind by logging operations. Like
Veazie, Iron River also suffered a disastrous fire in 1892. Of the hundred
buildings in town, seventy-two burned (Lund 1975, 78), but Iron River
did recover from the fire. Lumbering continued to be the primary livelihood
for the residents of this thriving community until the beginning of the
twentieth century. As time went on, the supply of great pines that were

so important to the early logging companies disappeared. The number of people able to eke out a living in the local woodland simultaneously decreased. The population of Iron River went from almost 2,400 at the height of the logging era in 1900 to less than 1,700 by 1910, a 30 percent decrease in just one decade. By 1912, the logging industry had further declined, and the last large mill shut down just one year before the business pulled out of town completely (Savage 1992). By the 1920 census, only 793 people lived in Iron River. Yet the community did survive and continues to evolve with the changing times.

Grantsburg

The third Pine Barrens community, Grantsburg, represents a somewhat different pattern of boom and bust associated with the timber industry. While Grantsburg did not rely as heavily on the cutting of timber to maintain economic stability, it did experience significant population decline when nearby timber resources were exhausted. Overall, Grantsburg was much quicker to recover the population losses it suffered during this time than was Iron River.

Grantsburg is another Pine Barrens community that emerged during the logging era in Wisconsin. Established in the mid-1860s, Grantsburg Township soon became a popular spot to settle. Grantsburg was the only township in existence in Burnett County prior to 1874. As with Iron River, it was largely due to the persistence of one individual that Grantsburg emerged when and where it did. Canute Anderson opened up a stopping place in Burnett County in 1854, just six miles south of where the village lies today. The original settlement consisted of a mill, a hotel, and a store. Although the exact location of the future county seat was debated, 160 acres had been acquired and platted by 1863 as the designated site for Grantsburg. Anderson, with the financial backing of Daniel Smith, erected a dam and sawmill in the chosen location that same year. The town was officially dedicated by 1865 but remained sparsely populated until many years later. Local and state politicians were continuously reorganizing local political boundaries. In 1865 the population of the whole county was 171; by 1870 it had increased to 706 (Crownhart 1965). Burnett County added more townships as population numbers increased, and as was stated above, the county eventually split in two.

By 1875, Grantsburg had three stores, a hotel, two sawmills, a shingle mill, a grist mill, two blacksmith shops, a saloon, a Methodist church, a

Lutheran church, and a school; new settlers were continuously moving to the area. The courthouse was completed in 1876 and burned down during a fire in 1888. Although some controversy erupted about where to rebuild the courthouse (and hence the county seat), Grantsburg prevailed for the time, and the new courthouse was built. Population in Grantsburg reached 241 by 1885 and the village incorporated in 1887 when the population reached 334, an increase of 38 percent over a period of just two years.

The railroad made it to Grantsburg by 1884 when turnaround tracks were completed. A good flow of passengers came daily on the train, and up to three trains per day carried freight shipments out of the town. Much of the freight consisted of wood logged in the vicinity. As the boom continued, Grantsburg became a thriving community. It wasn't long before the town housed a brick factory, two starch factories (potatoes were a successful crop at the time), a grass carpet factory (harvested from what is now Crex Meadows Wildlife Area), stockyards, an excelsior mill, a sash and door factory, and a paint factory. The Grantsburg train was nicknamed the Blueberry Special because of the large quantities of blueberries shipped out (2,773 bushels in one season) (Crownhart 1965). By the beginning of the twentieth century Grantsburg appeared to have all the makings of a securely established community: a variety of imports/exports as well as a diverse social structure and numerous employment opportunities.

THE MEANDERING PERIOD: A LOSS OF DIRECTION

During the early days of lumbering, logging companies considered the forests so cheap that they gave little attention to conservation. Instead, the Pine Barrens was clear-cut, stripped of its majestic white pines, and "mined" for lumber. The end of the logging era in northern Wisconsin brought many changes to the cutover region. The common rural development adage during this early settlement period was that the plow followed the ax. This tended to be the settlement pattern of many forested regions during the 1800s in U.S. history as they transitioned from timber toward agriculture. However, in the Northwoods, some communities failed to make the transition from logging to agriculture for a variety of reasons, not the least of which was poor soil and adverse climatic conditions (Kates 2001).

Many attempts were made to clear the land of stumps to make farming more accessible. Logging and colonization companies sold their land to hopeful immigrant farmers ready to capitalize on the productive promises of the land. However, clearing the land of cutover stumps proved to be an enormous challenge for many farmers. TNT was used as a final attempt to blast the stumps out of the ground, yet progress remained slow. Many people, such as Harry L. Russell, dean of agriculture at the University of Wisconsin, embraced the opportunity to bring agricultural development to the Pine Barrens region (Bawden 1997). The agricultural schools at the University of Wisconsin and Michigan State University embraced the opportunity to spread modern farming methods to new areas and to demonstrate the perceived capacity of contemporary techniques to make any land arable (Kates 2001). Farming in northern Wisconsin was successful in small, isolated pockets, yet all the effort put into promoting agriculture could not make the soil fertile and the climate suitable for large-scale success. Many of the farmers found it necessary to work in the remaining timber industry during the winter months to make ends meet. By the early 1920s, much of the cutover land had become tax delinquent or abandoned. Robert Gough in his book *Farming the Cutover* (1997) describes the plight of many forested regions turned agriculture in the 1920s to 1940s. He suggests this Northwoods region and its remaining people felt great uncertainty for their future. Towns like Veazie disappeared as logging ceased and farming failed. The region drifted without a clear picture of its future direction.

Many settlers left the area when agricultural pursuits proved to be futile. Poor soils, drought, difficult-to-remove stumps, rocks, and boulders, and a sudden decrease in demand for agricultural products after World War I contributed to agricultural failure in the north. Although there was some fluctuation in the population from 1920 to 1960, overall numbers declined throughout the region until the 1970s. For decades, out-migration occurred at an alarming rate; fewer than 16 percent of the original local farmers were still on the land in 1940 (Vogeler 1986). But a rediscovery of the Northwoods was soon to bring life back to region.

The Rediscovery Period: Capturing Their Amenity Assets

Northwestern Wisconsin traditionally had a production landscape dominated by forestry, fisheries, mining, and agriculture since the onset of Euro-American settlement. Yet since the 1930s, the region has been continuously reshaping itself into a consumption landscape. Many communities that once dotted the countryside are gone. Others that at one time had a strong economy based on extractive resources are a shell of their past, but a few are prospering. Throughout the book we return to communities in the Pine Barrens that have made the transition from a production landscape to a consumption landscape. We begin with Iron River and Grantsburg.

Iron River

The decline in population occurring in Iron River after the timber resources were gone indicated dire economic hardship for area residents. As discussed by Marchak (1983), Landis (1997), and Freudenburg (1992), so much of the local economy, infrastructure, and labor were tied up in the logging industry that when the resource failed, Iron River experienced the downfall of the classic boom and bust cycle seen in so many resource-dependent towns. When farming was promoted in Iron River and Bayfield County, it was dairy farming that took hold. In order to accommodate this new opportunity, several cheese factories and creameries were established. In 1925, locally raised capital built a stringless bean factory. As the community struggled to create an agricultural economy, hints of the future consumption landscape began to appear. Resorts and cottages were set up to accommodate the growth of local and nonlocal citizens' recreational pursuits. Several of the ninety-six lakes in the Iron River vicinity were touted as being well stocked with muskellunge, northern pike, and other varieties of fish. Clear-running trout streams were also a prominent attraction. The abundance of blueberries supported the celebration of annual blueberry festivals. These early recreational activities and an identity as a recreation destination laid the groundwork for the consumption landscape of the rediscovery period.

The institutional structure in Iron River was slowly diversifying. Churches of varying denominations, the Women's Temperance Union, a library, a sportsman's club, and a Boy Scout troop had been well established by the end of the second decade of rediscovery. Entertainment possibilities consisted of talent plays, card parties, motion pictures, dances, bands and singing groups, and other sporting events such as skating, curling, skiing, hockey, and bicycling. By 1920, new business establishments and organizations included a big pickle factory, a MacIntosh wagon factory, three churches, a laundry, the Iron River band, two banks, two lawyers, two dentists, two doctors, a funeral parlor, two drug stores, three department stores, thirty-eight saloons, and five hotels (*Iron River, Wisconsin Centennial* 1992).

Over the next several decades, both the pickle and wagon factory closed, and the number of dairy farms dropped dramatically. In the postwar years, the production landscape dwindled as recreation and tourism consumption

rose to prominence. As the twenty-first century approached, tourism accommodations within the community became a large part of the local economy. By 2001, the Iron River Chamber of Commerce list of businesses
included twenty-one lodging facilities, including two bed and breakfasts
and at least thirteen resorts. Retail businesses increased in number and
include espresso and Internet bars, art galleries, gift shops, a winery, sports
and recreation shops, and a bakery. New construction enables electrical
contractors, well drillers, real estate services, and excavators to stay in business. Iron River area tourist attractions also include canoe rentals, charter
fishing, riding stables, ski trails and hills, groomed snowmobile trails, bik-
ing trails, sleigh rides, a golf course, museums, art galleries and studios, and
a nearby casino.

As you drive through Iron River today, it is apparent that new construction is occurring at a rapid pace. Iron River is an easy commute to larger
urban centers because it is located along one of the main routes across
northern Wisconsin (U.S. Highway 2). The city of Ashland is located just
twenty-seven miles to the east, while the twin cities of Superior and Duluth
lie northwest about forty miles. The area's many lakes and close proximity to national, state, and county forests make it an attractive getaway
for seasonal residents as well as tourists passing through the region. Local
businesses including several private cottages, campgrounds, resorts, charter fishing boats, ATV rentals, upscale clothing boutiques, and a new medical center cater to tourists and seasonal residents (Iron River Chamber of
Commerce 2008). Iron River began its life as a community dependent on
timber extraction for its economic livelihood. The community has since
evolved a broader, more diverse economy directed at the preservation and
recreation consumption of its natural amenities—the lakes and forests surrounding it.

Grantsburg

The village of Grantsburg has also undergone significant changes over the
last century. The census estimates that Grantsburg grew by 10.84 percent
from 1990 to 2000. Community planners have drawn up numerous goals
and recommendations in an effort to ensure sound economic and developmental growth. Burnett County is one of the fastest growing counties in
northwestern Wisconsin (exceeded in growth only by Sawyer and Washburn Counties). Much of the population growth has taken place to the
northeast of Grantsburg in the lakes district. The county administrator

estimates that the summertime population of Burnett County is forty thousand—almost three times higher than the year-round population.

Much of Grantsburg's growth has been attributed to its proximity to Minneapolis and St. Paul and to its manufacturing base. Various manufacturing facilities in Grantsburg produce cheese, stainless equipment, truss rafters, machined parts, medical equipment washers, trailers and fabricated custom metal, wooden shutters, hydraulic and pneumatic couplers, and plastic injection molds. The ability of Grantsburg officials to attract manufacturers appears to play an instrumental role in the economic stability of the community.

Tourism also plays a major part in the economy of the area. The Department of Commerce estimates visitors spent $21.9 million in Burnett County in 1997. Various attractions to the area include canoeing and camping along the St. Croix Scenic Riverway, hiking, biking, skiing, horseback riding, ATV and snowmobile trails, and several designated state wildlife areas where bird watching and hunting are important activities. Various other water sports such as boating, swimming, water-skiing, jet-skiing, and tubing are promoted on the many local lakes.

Services for year-round residents are readily available. The elderly population increased 1.8 percent from 1980 to 1990, and projections show this trend continuing. Like other natural amenity-rich regions, Grantsburg tends to attract an older population, which has a substantial effect on the types of services offered in the community. Hospitals, clinics, and related services are an important component of the services offered in the region. Grantsburg now boasts only one forest resources company in contrast to its numerous resorts and private cottages, several day spas, and several restaurants (Grantsburg Chamber of Commerce 2008).

With the post–World War II recreational boom, the Pine Barrens region became one of Wisconsin's major recreational destinations, feeding the rediscovery and renewed appreciation of natural amenity attributes (Vogeler 1986, 87). A number of factors contributed to the increase in population during this time period. Voss and Fuguitt (1979) conducted a survey of residents in northern Wisconsin and found that many families relocated to the area to enjoy the abundant natural amenities. The desire to leave city life, lower costs of living, relocating back to family and friends, or taking up residence in a second home were common reasons to move to northern Wisconsin. This reshaping of the population and community identity has led to a redefinition of the natural resources and development of a consumption landscape. It is this fourth era of rediscovery that is our book's primary focus. We use this era to describe the new relationships of people and land in northwestern Wisconsin.

Through the years, the people and forests of northern Wisconsin have changed. There has been a transformation of communities, the social environment of the countryside, and the natural environment of the Northwoods. The influence of extractive industries on community affairs has given way to an economy based on capturing the aesthetic quality of forests, lakes, and rivers. In turn this has had far-reaching effects on population structure and organization of communities. Today, recent migrants to the region, many of whom are retirees and seasonal residents, play major roles in the affairs of many of these communities. The cultural landscape of the Northwoods has been transformed from a production landscape of forestry and agriculture to a consumption landscape capturing the natural amenity assets of the region. Within this context, we examine the rediscovery and transformation of the Northwoods Pine Barrens and patterns on the land. Bawden perhaps best describes the current state of the Northwoods:

> In what category, then, does the northwoods fall—nature or culture? The question truly cannot be answered in these terms. People and the environment together have shaped this place: the lumberjack cutting the forests, the farmer pulling the stumps, the forester planting the trees, and the urbanite traveling along Highway 51. In each relationship there is an exchange between society and nature, each transforming the other. (Bawden 1997, 466)

This society-nature connection guides us as we seek to answer the question of what role the seasonal residents and recent migrants play in transforming the definition and institutional structure of communities and the ecology of the consumption landscape.

chapter 3

A National Perspective on the Reinvention of Rural Areas

I N RECENT DECADES, THERE HAS BEEN an ebb and flow of population and changing demographic composition of communities as some parts of rural America have been rediscovered. In this chapter, we examine three national trends in rural community change: in-migration, rural housing growth, and growth in seasonal homeownership. These three major sociodemographic trends are contributing significant community change in many rural areas rich in natural amenities. Seasonal homeownership is part of a broader transformation of rural communities as they also face new migrants, particularly urbanites and retirees, but we also explore the unique features of seasonal homeownership that differentiate it from other changes in natural amenity communities. Further, we show that these changes are the result of a new relationship to natural resources in rural regions as they shift from extractive industries to natural amenity development.

Since industrialization, the predominant population trend has been urbanization and a declining rural population (Johnson 1999; Ravenstein 1876). Demographers and other rural social scientists expected this trend to continue indefinitely, driven by increased farm size and mechanization in extractive industries and the attraction of urban lifestyle and economic opportunities. It was a surprise, then, when some contemporary rural communities started to grow and experience new in-migration. During the 1960s, the rural population loss of earlier decades began to slow, and there was evidence of new migration into U.S. nonmetropolitan counties. However, young adults continued to leave nonmetropolitan areas in large numbers, driven by the same economic and social factors of earlier decades. Instead, new arrivals of older adults and retirees into nonmetropolitan counties led the reversal of the population decline. Detailed analysis by Johnson and Fuguitt (2000) revealed that very little of this change occurred within counties dominated by farming. Instead, the new in-migration occurred primarily in nonmetropolitan counties with recreation economies and in "commuting counties" where 15 percent or more of the workers commuted to metropolitan counties for employment.

This trend continued through the 1970s, with even higher rates of in-migration for many nonmetropolitan areas. For the first time in recent history, rural areas of the United States experienced growth rates higher than those of cities (Fuguitt 1985). While out-migration was still present for young adults (those in their twenties), this population loss had declined significantly. The new migration flow from urban to rural areas was excitedly called the "rural renaissance," "rural turn around," or "rural rebound" (Johnson and Fuguitt 2000). Following a brief decline in the 1980s, the 1990s witnessed a return to the rural migration and growth of the 1970s. Natural increase from births accounted for little of the population growth during recent decades. Instead, out-migration away from nonmetropolitan areas slowed, and urban to rural migration brought new residents to rural communities (McGranahan 1999).

Several factors were at work in this new rural migration trend. Suburban and rural counties began to diversify their employment structure, relying less on resource extraction as their sole economic base. Innovations in transportation and communication such as the dawn of telecommuting also helped diminish the "friction of distance," giving companies and individuals more flexibility regarding their location. But most important was the increased importance of non-economic factors such as the natural environment and quality of life on migration decisions, attracting migrants to rural areas that are rich in scenic and recreational amenities (Beale and Johnson 1998; Brown et al. 1997; Frey and Johnson 1998; Johnson and Beale 2002; Johnson and Fuguitt 2000; McGranahan 1999; A. Nelson 1992; A. Nelson and Dueker 1990; Rudzitis 1999; Schwarzweller 1979).

IMPACTS OF POPULATION CHANGE: DIFFERENT VALUES, CULTURES CLASH

Rural communities have often experienced significant social conflict as a result of shifting to a non-extractive relationship to natural resources and the integration of new migrants. In this section we review the literature examining some challenging social impacts of new rural populations, including conflicts over natural resource use and a lack of community cohesion.

For many new migrants, the preservation of rural landscapes—preventing development—is a critical natural resource issue. Halfacree and Boyle (1998) argue that new residents commodify rural places for their natural amenities and aesthetics, leading to conflict over natural resources in the "post-productivist countryside." Newcomers prefer to preserve idealized landscapes of rolling hills, farms, forests, and open spaces (Halfacree and Boyle 1998; Halseth 1998; P. Nelson 2001; Shumway and Lethbridge 1998; Smutny 2002; Walker and Fortmann 2003). In contrast, many long-time residents support new growth and development, seeing growth as a means to provide jobs for themselves and their children (P. Nelson 2001; Spain 1993; Walker and Fortmann 2003). Many rural communities struggle over the landscape and natural resources, with those residents who support productive and extractive uses of the land increasingly at odds with those who support aesthetic and consumptive uses of the land.

Conflict over management priorities of public lands and forests reflects similar differences. New residents often hold negative views of extractive management policies and push for changes in public management priorities that favor preservation, the environment, and recreation (Egan and Luloff 2000; P. Nelson 2001; Rudzitis 1999). These different approaches to natural resources serve as a proxy for tensions in rural communities including class conflict, cultural conflict, and struggles for control over local decision making.

Communities on the outskirts of an urban area, otherwise called "exurbia" or "the fringe," are particularly contested and conflicted (Audirac 1999; T. Daniels 1999; Halfacree 1997; Halfacree and Boyle 1998; A. Nelson and Dueker 1990). These areas, while rural in appearance, are inextricably tied to their neighboring urban center as the pressures from population and economic growth extend from central cities and suburbs. The conflict between urban and rural orientations of residents can support extreme conflict over aesthetic versus extractive uses of natural resources.

Along with such conflicts over natural resource values and development, new migrants often have difficulty socially integrating into rural communities. Salamon's *Newcomers to Old Towns* (2003) examines the destructive impacts of what she describes as the "onslaught of suburbanization" on rural communities. Whereas long-term residents define community in terms of social relations, newcomers view community in terms of commodities such as "good schools," "safe streets," and "open space." Newcomers, according to Salamon, are not socially or economically connected to the larger community. Instead, newcomers create parallel communities including only other newcomers, with little interaction and few shared values, customs, or norms with long-term residents.

Walker and Fortmann's (2003) study of Nevada County, California, offers another view of a rural community struggling with newcomers and a transition from a production to a consumption landscape. Walker and Fortmann describe the evolving relations of class and power that are central to conflicting visions of the landscape and the community. Newcomers to Nevada County have "aestheticized" the landscape and want future development to be based on recreation and services. This conflicts with the long-term residents and traditional powerbrokers who depend on extractive uses of the land (forestry, ranching, and agriculture). Conflicts over land use planning and local politics have become a proxy for class conflict between new migrants and long-term residents, and the inability of local residents to create a shared vision of the landscape has created bitter divisions, rivalries, and conflict within the community. The in-migration of new residents has weakened community solidarity in Nevada County.

Like Salamon (2003) and Walker and Fortmann (2003), Peter Nelson (2001) examines the ways in which residents of four rapidly growing rural communities in the western United States have adjusted to the changes occurring in their communities due to rural migration. Each of the four communities experienced rapid population growth as well as economic shifts away from resource extraction to services, niche manufacturing, and tourism. New residents, largely middle and upper class, are "colonizing" these rural regions and shifting the emphasis in land management from production to preservation. The arrival of new residents, who favor amenities and preservation, changes the identity of long-term residents, communities, and the surrounding landscape. Demographic and economic transformations have led to a loss of shared community values and community identity and hampered efforts to organize and act collectively (P. Nelson 2001).

Other community studies have also found residents of amenity-rich regions divided over resource management and community strategies. For example, Graber (1974) finds that new residents in the mountain town of Georgetown, Colorado, are much more supportive of a historic preservation ordinance than long-time residents. Similarly, Cockerham and Blevins (1977) find newcomers in Jackson Hole, Wyoming, to be more supportive of land use planning than their long-time counterparts. Similar support for growth controls and preservation policies from new residents has been found in the exurbs of San Francisco and Los Angeles (Dubbink 1984) and rural Virginia (Spain 1993).

However, results from some community studies comparing the attitudes of newcomers and long-time residents toward natural resource management are more mixed, sometimes finding conflict and other times finding general agreement among residents. For example, Smith and Krannich (2000) find differences in environmental attitudes between new and long-time residents in only one of three study communities in Utah. Similarly, studies of the rural rebound conducted in the North Central and Upper Great Lake states have found few differences between new and long-time residents in attitudes toward issues such as population growth and the environment (Blahna 1990; Sofranko and Fliegel 1980; Voss 1980). Blahna (1990) finds little support for a culture clash in his study of rural Michigan communities, as there are few differences in environmental attitudes between new and long-term residents. Sofranko and Fliegel (1980) find universal support for economic development from new and long-time residents alike. They do, however, find contrasting views on raising taxes to improve schools and other local services. Interestingly, it is newcomers from other rural communities who support raising taxes to improve schools, not migrants from urban areas as hypothesized. In addition, Fliegel, Sofranko, and Glasgow (1981) find all residents held strong attitudes favoring growth and development. These studies offer a view of communities that have survived the transformation to consumption landscapes and are built on shared natural resource and community values.

RURAL HOUSING PATTERNS: THE GROWTH OF SEASONAL HOUSING IN THE COUNTRYSIDE

While the literature is replete with discussions of interaction between newcomers and long-term residents, in the case of northwestern Wisconsin and many other amenity-rich rural regions, migration alone does not explain all of the transformations that communities are experiencing. Many rural communities have also experienced dramatic growth in the number and concentration of seasonal or vacation homes. Growth in seasonal homes and the arrival of seasonal residents is another important driver of community change and growth, and an understanding of American rural change is incomplete without a discussion of seasonal housing trends.

Second-home ownership has boomed in the past several decades, focused primarily in nonmetropolitan counties offering recreational natural resources or proximity to major population centers (Beale and Johnson 1998; Coppock 1977c; Marcouiller et al. 1996; Robertson 1977; Wolfe 1977). Urban residents seeking relaxation, recreation, and an escape from frenzied lifestyles have relocated to rural areas, purchased second homes, and flooded small communities. Across the United States, seasonal homes provide an often overlooked but significant portion of the housing stock in many rural communities. Seasonal homes, also commonly referred to as cottages, vacation homes, or recreational homes, are private homes used by their owners on weekends, vacations, or holidays (Green and Clendenning 2003). The U.S. Census Bureau defines them as vacant units used or intended for use only in certain seasons, for weekends, or other occasional use throughout the year (US Census Bureau 2002).

The number of seasonal homes in the United States increased dramatically over the second half of the twentieth century. Between 1960 and 2000, the national number of seasonal homes increased by almost 77 percent from 2,024,381 homes to 3,578,718 homes. Wisconsin experienced a similar increase in seasonal homes, adding 61 percent more homes between 1960 and 2000 (rising from 88,130 to 142,313 seasonal homes). When compared to other states, Wisconsin has a high absolute number of seasonal homes (seventh highest number of seasonal homes of any state) and also a high percentage of seasonal homes. Slightly more than 6 percent of all its homes are seasonal compared to 3.4 percent for the United States as a whole, giving Wisconsin the eighth highest percentage of housing units classified as seasonal (U.S. Census Bureau 2001a, 2002). Seasonal homes in Wisconsin are largely concentrated in the upper third of the state (see Marcouiller et al. 1996).

IMPACTS OF SEASONAL HOUSING

While it is often assumed that seasonal homeowners replicate the conflicts and struggles associated with migration of new residents, some recent studies suggest that seasonal housing has unique patterns and impacts. In the following sections we review the literature on seasonal homeownership and its impacts on host communities including divergent development priorities, conflicting environmental attitudes, and social friction. We follow this with a discussion of previous studies of northern Wisconsin and others who suggest that the anticipated conflicts between seasonal and permanent homeowners may have been overstated.

Seasonal Homeownership and Economic Development

There are both positive and negative economic impacts of second-home development on host communities. Perhaps more than any other issue related to seasonal homes, this has received attention from a variety of disciplines and the popular media over concerns including the fiscal burden on local governments, rural gentrification, and opposing planning and development goals of permanent and seasonal residents.

One major economic concern has been the service burden placed on host communities by seasonal residents. Second-home development can require substantial inputs by local governments in utilities (sewer, water, and electrical), roads, police and fire protection, health and welfare services, and general government administration (American Society 1976, 62). When private water or sewer systems fail, as has been documented in second-home communities in Virginia, Pennsylvania, and Colorado, local county planning boards and health agencies must bear the costs of dealing with contamination and rebuilding (63). The American Society of Planning Officials determined that short-term economic gains brought by second-home development, if not properly regulated by planning, would be dwarfed by the long-term costs of support, particularly if recreational homes became primary residences. Deller, Marcouiller, and Green (1997) documented the many costs to local governments caused by recreational housing development, including the development of second homes. They concluded that the revenues and expenditures for local governments resulting from recreational housing just "break even." While recreational development does not drain valuable financial resources from local governments, it is also not a source of fiscal revival. An inconsistent seasonal spending pattern is a pressing concern for second-home communities (Stewart and Stynes 2006) since local businesses experience significant declines during the "low season."

Concern about increasing property values also figures in much discussion of the economic impacts of seasonal homes. For several decades, increased property values resulting from the expansion of seasonal housing in rural areas, particularly newly built second homes, have been at the center of the controversy surrounding second homes and homeowners. From Wyoming to New York, Belgium, and France, concern has mounted about the negative impacts of increasing property values on host communities (Albarre 1977; Bielckus 1977; Clout 1977; Jensen and Field 2004; Visser 2004). Critics argue that increasing property values support rural out-migration and inflate prices beyond the reach of permanent, long-term residents. Second-home development in economically depressed areas or areas with low homeownership rates have particularly negative outcomes for host communities (Visser 2004; Henshal 1977).

Similar to studies of newcomer conflict, many studies also highlight the long-term concerns surrounding divergent development priorities held by permanent and seasonal residents (Coppock 1977b; Deller, Marcouiller, and Green 1997; Green et al. 1996; Jensen and Field 2004; Williams and Van Patten 2006). While permanent residents typically demonstrate a desire for diverse economic development to ensure their livelihood and the survival of their community, seasonal residents frequently prioritize maintaining the status quo and limiting development to protect privacy and aesthetic beauty. Coppock captures this attitude in the Commuter's Doxology (1977a, 152):

O Lord, we thank Thee that Thy grace
Hath brought us to this lovely place
And now, O Lord, we humbly pray
Thou wilt all others keep away

Rural Housing Growth and the Environment

The environmental impacts of seasonal housing development represent another major concern. Early studies of second homes identified environmental concerns about landscape alteration from increased use, pollution, and erosion (Albarre 1977). The concentration of second homes in amenity-rich areas and their connection to recreation activities has been thoroughly documented (Marcouiller et al. 1996; Robertson 1977; Wolfe 1977). But a presence in amenity-rich areas also means many second homes are near environmentally fragile landscapes.

A lack of environmental regulations and restrictions surrounding rapid development of second homes has been a major problem. Romeril (1984) argues that environmental degradation occurs because outside developers have no concern for local environments and therefore could not be expected to make protective decisions. Gartner (1987) finds that even in settings with fairly strict environmental regulations, most residents and developers are unaware of existing laws, and enforcement is virtually non-existent. While the problems associated with a lack of regulation are well documented, host communities face difficult choices. Second-home and recreational development may lead to environmental degradation, but it can also promise much-needed economic opportunities for depressed areas. Local communities may not be willing to risk creating and enforcing environmental restrictions when doing so could discourage developers from moving into the area (Eastwood and Carter 1981; Humphries 1986; Stroud 1983).

Several major environmental studies have highlighted the impact of seasonal and recreational homes on coastal and other water ecosystems. Since water resources are attractive for development of recreational and seasonal homes (Chubb 1989; Chubb and Chubb 1981; Perkins and Thorns 2006; Selwood and Tonts 2006; Stynes and Holecek 1982), water pollution can become a problem as seasonal housing expands. Studies by Gonen (1981), Dearden (1983), and Samra (1984) draw attention to the degradation of coastline estuaries, damage to beaches, and decline of water quality in the Mediterranean, British Columbia, and the English coast, respectively. Each of these studies places responsibility for this environmental damage squarely on the shoulders of unregulated recreational development, of which second homes constitute a major portion. Issues of water pollution and degradation are particularly relevant to northwestern Wisconsin, which is covered in small and medium lakes.

Seasonal housing development is also linked to sewer and septic failure and resulting contamination of groundwater (Ragatz 1977). Such contamination can lead to high levels of eutrophication, a problem exacerbated by runoff from domestic lawn care fertilizers (T. Groves 1986; Stedman and Hammer 2006). These other environmental concerns drive much debate of second homes and their impacts on their host community (American Society 1976; Coppock 1977a; Cox and Mair 1988; Green et al. 1996; *Private Seasonal Housing* 1966; Jackson 1974; Shellito 2006).

Seasonal Homeownership and a New Social Order

Aside from fiscal and environmental impacts of seasonal housing development, it is important to understand the social impact of seasonal residency on rural communities. Understanding motivations for second homeownership is one component of appreciating these impacts, since desires and expectations of seasonal residents shape how they engage with their new community. A desire for recreation and relaxation motivates most second homeownership (American Society 1976; Clendenning and Field 2005; Girard and Gartner 1993; Green et al. 1996; Jensen and Field 2004; Marcouiller et al. 1996). Seasonal residents in the United States tend to make their decisions concerning if and where to buy a second home based upon the recreation potential of the host community and the aesthetic beauty of the area. The desire for escape from the pressures of modernity is an often-cited motivation for the purchase of a second home (McHugh 2007; McIntyre, Williams, and McHugh 2006b; Williams and Van Patten 2006).

Also important to social impacts of second-home development is the fact that seasonal residents often come from very different backgrounds than their permanent counterparts and may reside in a permanent community substantially different from that of their seasonal home. Of particular concern in European and international second homeownership has been growth in number of foreign second homeowners (Coppock 1977c; Gustafson 2002; Henshal 1977; Marsh and Griffiths 2006; Periainen 2006; Romeril 1984). When seasonal residents reside permanently in a different country, problems related to different customs, beliefs, backgrounds, and priorities may be exacerbated. Differences between permanent and seasonal homeowners can lead to social tensions and divisions in the host community.

Such differences are not limited to situations of international second homeownership, however. Jordan (1980), in his study of cottagers in Vermont, found high levels of social tension in the host communities and significant concerns among permanent residents about a loss of identity and independence. Permanent residents expressed concern that seasonal residents from urban areas did not share a "rural identity" important to the community, and that their presence was leading to a loss of "historical and cultural traditions" (Girard and Gartner 1993). The fear of losing community identity and values has been echoed in many studies of recreational and seasonal housing (Allen et al. 1988; Doxey 1975).

Seasonal Homeownership: Questioning the Conflict

However, some recent empirical work has questioned this often-assumed conflict and divergence of values between seasonal and permanent residents. In their study of the values of permanent, new migrant, and seasonal homeowners in New Zealand, McIntyre and Pavlovich (2006) find a surprising similarity between the groups. The three groups of residents did diverge significantly, however, on their attitudes toward tourism and continued housing development. Many recent studies also recognize the important role that desires for "rootedness" and a deep connection to a place play in motivating second-home purchases (Gustafson 2006; Stedman 2006; Williams and Van Patten 2006). Second homes can be more than simply a place to flee demands and seek recreation. They can serve as a true *home* that provides meaning, place, and community for owners. This desire for community and an attachment to the local community can motivate seasonal home purchases (Jaakson 1986; Perkins and Thorns 2006; Yoffe 2000). Indeed, the uniqueness of the communities formed around seasonal homes and their importance to members can support a strong commitment to host communities (Turner and Turner 1982; Yoffee 2000).

There is also some evidence that seasonal housing does offer economic benefits to host communities. Seasonal home development can bring much needed economic activity into depressed areas, from construction jobs and sale of building materials to generating employment through spending during visits. Early reports from Fine and Werner (1966) estimated that within Wisconsin, private seasonal housing contributed $75 million to the state economy through revenue from land purchases, building costs, travel, and services. A later study by Marcouiller et al. (1996, i) found that seasonal homeowners spent an average of $6,000 per year on items directly used in or attributed to their seasonal home. Although recognizing that many of the employment options created are of limited social prestige and economic potential, Visser argues that "second home development . . . is a productive resource" (2004, 270), offering a variety of economic linkages. As rural communities struggle to survive depopulation, the decline of extractive industries, and general economic hardship, second-home development can offer much-needed employment opportunities and customers (Coppock 1977c; Green and Clendenning 2003; Green et al. 1996; Jordan 1980).

Studies of Seasonal Residents in the Wisconsin Northwoods

Various studies examine seasonal homeownership specifically within the Wisconsin Northwoods. Williams and Van Patten (2006) examined the Hayward Lakes region of northern Wisconsin, an area bordering our study area on the east. Exploring the motivations for second homeownership in the region, they find second homes provide an important escape from modernity but also help create identity and rootedness within the modern world. Second homes provide their owners with a place to gather, create togetherness, and establish a sense of connection and continuity to a mythic place. The development of second homes only complicates many struggles over the direction and development of the Hayward Lakes region. Like many seasonal home destinations, the region struggles to lure capital and development opportunities while maintaining the natural allure of the area.

Problems of contemporary growth conflict with an idealized past of "dwelling with nature" (Williams and Van Patten 2006).

Divergent development priorities were also evident in the central to eastern areas of the Northwoods (Green et al. 1996). Offering a larger regional perspective on the distributions and effects of second homes in the Upper Great Lakes region, Shellito (2006) finds that two key factors shape the distribution of second homes in the region: the availability of recreational and natural areas and the proximity and accessibility to large population centers.

Stedman's numerous studies of second homeowners in the Vilas County area of northeastern Wisconsin (2002, 2003, 2006, 2008) use a sense of place and place attachment perspective to understand how second homeowners construct meaning and identity from their second homes. Rather than assuming negative attitudes toward, or effects on, the local community, Stedman questions second homeowners about the meanings their second home holds and the connections they have to the area. In contrast to many studies told only from the perspective of permanent residents, Stedman finds that second homeowners are actually very attached to their new places and that they value their local communities. Stedman (2006) also finds that seasonal homeowners who use their home frequently are more similar to permanent residents than infrequent seasonal residents in terms of community values, political involvement, and social networks. As discussed in chapters 5 and 6, we also find this in our study of northwestern Wisconsin. However, Stedman's study region of northern Wisconsin differs from ours in that the majority of second homeowners in the area (63.2 percent in his sample) have a primary residence within Wisconsin, and a significant minority (24.7 percent in his sample) are from Illinois (2006, 136). In contrast, the northwestern area of Wisconsin draws second-home owners heavily from Minnesota (65 percent of our sample are from Minnesota), especially the Minneapolis and St. Paul metropolitan area (64 percent of our sample).

CONCLUSION

In this chapter we highlighted new trends in rural population change and housing development. In-migration from urban areas, retirees building homes in the countryside, and second-home development are important drivers of social and environmental change in rural communities. Many natural amenity-rich rural communities are being transformed by the introduction of new and diverse residents with different attitudes toward development and natural resources. The composition of rural communities is changing and ushering in significant social transformations such as a shift to an aesthetic understanding of natural resources and social tensions around rural identity. Vacation homeownership in rural areas has increased dramatically and is further transforming rural communities. Seasonal housing development may bring with it some of the same economic, environmental, and social unrest of new migrants, although some new studies are questioning this assumption. What is apparent from the growing body of empirical studies is that rural communities are being transformed as their relationship to their natural environment shifts away from extractive development. This is particularly evident in natural amenity-rich rural landscapes: those areas with abundant forests, lakes, and public lands where growth in population and seasonal housing is transforming the social structure of rural communities and patterns of land use.

chapter 4

The Regional Context of Reinvention of a Rural Area

W HILE RURAL AMERICAN COMMUNITIES have recently transformed significantly in terms of population, environment, and social organization at the national level (as discussed in the previous chapter), northwestern Wisconsin has undergone its own unique changes. In this chapter we move from a national picture of rural change and direct our focus on a small subregion—the Pine Barrens of northwestern Wisconsin and our study area within the region (see figure 4.1). This region has experienced large changes in demographics: first in population decline and then growth. Changes also include out-migration of youth, in-migration of adult workers and retirees, new housing development, and an upswing in seasonal homeownership. Pine Barrens communities are changing as new people move in, lumber mills close, and tourism and vacation homes grow.

Since the 1990s, population growth in the area has spawned new economic activities and created more diversified employment opportunities. Wisconsin's *State Comprehensive Outdoor Recreation Plan (SCORP)* indicates that as a region, the five Pine Barrens counties of Bayfield, Burnett, Douglas, Polk, and Washburn have experienced a 22.37 percent population increase since 1950 and a 28 percent population increase since 1970.[1] This growth was not, however, evenly distributed. During these fifty years,

1. Data used for analysis in this chapter are drawn from the United States Decennial Census (Summary File 1 and Summary File 3) for the years 1970, 1980, 1990, and 2000 (2000a, 2000b). The historical Census data were derived from the Geo-Lytics Census software packages for 1970 and 1980; 1990 and 2000 data were obtained through the Census Bureau's web resource, American Fact Finder.

Polk County had the highest growth (66 percent) while Douglas County lost 7 percent of its population. Douglas County is the northern most county in the state and most distant from the Twin Cities metropolitan area, factors that decreased its natural amenity appeal. With the exception of Douglas County, each of the other counties experienced its most dramatic growth during the 1970s. This reflected the beginning of the rural rebound introduced in the previous chapter as well as the beginning of new "quality of life" and natural amenity migration in the Northwoods. The population spiked again in the early 1990s, mirroring the national rural

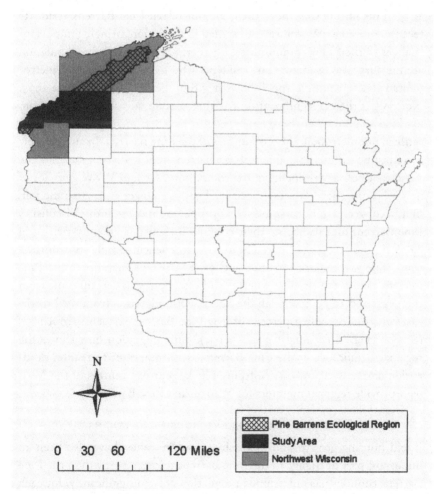

FIGURE 4.1. Map of the study area

rebound. Douglas County also appears to be experiencing this resurgence demonstrating positive growth throughout the 1990s and positive estimates since 2000 (*SCORP* 2005). The population waves of the Pine Barrens mirror the trends seen in rural counties throughout the United States.

Most of the population growth in the Pine Barrens comes from in-migration of new residents. The concentration of new in-migrants from out of state is an important variable to demonstrate the growth of new rural constituencies and significant community change in rural areas (Winkler et al. 2007). In total, 11 percent of the population in the five Pine Barrens counties (over five years of age) moved into the area from out of state since 1995. This means that more than one out of ten Pine Barrens residents recently moved to Wisconsin and settled in the region, bringing important changes to their new communities. Further, 8.7 percent of the population are not just new residents, but residents who have moved from a metropolitan area to a nonmetropolitan area within the Pine Barrens since 1995. Not only is there a significant flow of out-of-state migrants to the region, but also 80 percent of those new residents have left metropolitan areas to settle in nonmetropolitan communities of the Pine Barrens. In an interview a county board member in the Pine Barrens repeatedly emphasized the significance of new residents in the community, saying: "We've got a lot of new folks now, new retirees especially. They're younger and active and join in a lot of recreation pursuits." New people are moving into Wisconsin's Pine Barrens and reshaping their communities just as amenity-rich rural communities across the United States are experiencing similar transformations. The vast majority (73 percent) of out-of-state migrants to the Pine Barrens came from elsewhere in the Midwest. Fourteen percent came from the West and 10 percent from the South, with migration from the Northeast constituting only 3 percent of new Pine Barrens residents from 1995 to 2000 (U.S. Decennial Census 2000c). This migration flow shows the regional significance of the Pine Barrens as an important recreation destination and natural amenity hotspot. The large urban centers of the Midwest provide regional migrants for Wisconsin's Pine Barrens.

EMERGING PINE BARRENS HOUSING PATTERNS

Rapid housing growth and increasing property values have also been an important part of change in the Pine Barrens. Housing growth in the Pine Barrens counties has outstripped population growth significantly: for each additional person in the Pine Barrens from 1970 to 2000, more than four houses were built during the same time period (*SCORP* 2005). This disparity between population and housing growth is a result of the growth of seasonal homes in the area. Like population growth, housing development has also been variable across time and space. The highest levels of housing development occurred in the 1970s, in Burnett and Washburn Counties (*SCORP* 2005). Developers moved into the area in force, expanding vacation homes into previously isolated rural communities. During every decade, each county's housing growth has been significantly higher than its population growth, with the exception of the 1990s (*SCORP* 2005). The growth in vacation housing in the Pine Barrens follows national trends of housing development in amenity-rich rural areas.

Clearly, much of this housing development has been for the seasonal housing market. Though cottages and resorts along the lakeshores of northern Wisconsin date to the beginning of the twentieth century, lakeshore development has risen dramatically since the 1950s. The Wisconsin Department of Natural Resources (DNR) estimated that the number of shoreline dwellings increased by over 200 percent between 1960 and 1995 (Wisconsin DNR 1996, 2000). A strong postwar economy and an improved road system made northern Wisconsin more accessible to an urban population that could afford to build second homes or stay in lakeside resorts (Kates 2001).

Wisconsin has a higher concentration of seasonal homes than both the nation and the Midwest region. In 1990, just over 7 percent of Wisconsin's housing units were for seasonal use, a concentration that remained relatively stable through 2000 (*SCORP* 2005). This means that seasonal housing is more than twice as prevalent in Wisconsin as nationally, and it constitutes a significant percentage of recent housing and housing growth. Throughout the five Pine Barrens counties, seasonal housing units have more than quadrupled (417 percent increase) since 1950. Since 1990, the concentration of seasonal housing has declined as a result of their conversion into full-time homes, but recreational and seasonal housing remains an important characteristic of the Pine Barrens region (ibid.). Overall, more than one in four homes in the region were occupied only seasonally. Mirroring the general housing trends, Burnett and Washburn Counties have the highest levels of seasonal housing in the region (see figure 4.2). As discussed in the previous chapter, seasonal housing brings a host of concerns and changes to rural communities such as new and different residents, increasing fiscal burden on local and county governments, and environmental threats.

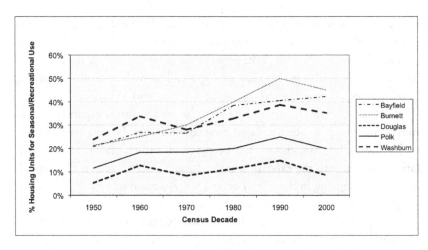

FIGURE 4.2. Seasonal housing by county (data from *SCORP* 2005)

The rise in housing values is an important issue in rural communities with high seasonal homeownership. Winkler et al. (2007) also determined that the percentage of owner-occupied housing units valued over $200,000 could be used as a statistical indicator of transformations in rural housing markets. A comparison of the median value of owner-occupied housing with the concentration of housing units valued over $200,000 makes it clear that there is a substantial amount of stratification in the housing market in the Pine Barrens area (see table 4.1). Housing stratification can lead to higher property tax burdens for residents and tensions in the community.

The rapid housing development in Pine Barrens communities has also dramatically increased the housing density in each of the counties (*SCORP* 2005). All five counties have experienced significant increases in housing density, with Polk, Bayfield, and Washburn Counties more than doubling

TABLE 4.1. Housing values by county

County	Percentage above $200,000	Median value ($)
Bayfield	4	87,500
Burnett	4	84,800
Douglas	2	70,800
Polk	7	100,200
Washburn	5	84,600

SOURCE: U.S. Census Bureau 2000b.

their housing density since 1950 and Burnett County tripling its housing density during the same period. Housing density is an important concern for communities seeking to preserve their rural character, especially when these open spaces are a key rural trait.

New Employment and New Economies in a Natural Amenity Region

General shifts in the employment structure of the Pine Barrens and changing relationships with natural resources are associated with these population and housing changes. In 2000, the tourism industry employed approximately 12 percent of the population in the Pine Barrens region (U.S. Decennial Census 2000b). This is remarkably high in a region previously dominated by extractive resource dependency and industries such as timber, agriculture, and mining. In the Pine Barrens, there are now more than five times as many adults employed in the food and accommodations sector as in the extractive industries (U.S. Census Bureau 2007). In the 2000 census, employment in tourism-related industries (food, recreation, entertainment, accommodations) was more than twice the employment in extractive industries (agriculture, fishing, hunting, mining) (U.S. Decennial Census 2000b). As employment in agriculture and forestry declined, service and tourism employment expanded rapidly. Pine Barrens communities have undergone an economic transformation reflecting their community transformations as they have shifted from traditional extractive industries to natural amenity development.

Employment in the financial, insurance, rental, and real estate (FIRE) sector of the economy further reflects the changing economy of the region (see table 4.2). Employment in this sector includes real estate developers and other services associated with housing development such as mortgages and loans. High employment in this sector is tied to rapid housing growth and development in rural communities (Winkler et al. 2007). While the levels of employment in this area are not as dramatic as those of tourism, it is still an important sector of employment in an area previously characterized by high levels of traditional resource dependency and extractive industry employment.

The Pine Barrens in Depth

In this book, we examine more specifically the portions of the Pine Barrens region that lie within Washburn and Burnett Counties. We chose these

TABLE 4.2. Employment by industry

County	Percentage employed in extractive industry	Percentage employed in FIRE sector	Percentage employed in tourism industry
Bayfield	6	4	13
Burnett	4	3	11
Douglas	1	6	10
Polk	5	4	6
Washburn	5	4	9

SOURCE: U.S. Census Bureau 2000b.

two counties as our case study because of their remarkably high levels of seasonal housing and because they represent the major trends of rural transformation. Both counties have experienced rapid population growth and second-home development. During the 1990s, Burnett County's population increased by 20 percent while Washburn County's population increased by 16 percent compared to Wisconsin's statewide population increase of 10 percent (*SCORP* 2005). Population growth was largely due to in-migration as both counties experienced negative rates of natural increase during the 1990s (i.e., the number of deaths in the two counties was greater than the number of births) (*SCORP* 2005).

Both Burnett and Washburn Counties have a significant portion of their population over sixty-five years of age, demonstrating the significance of their role as a retirement destination (see table 4.3). The percentage of the national population over the age of sixty-five is 12.1 percent, a concentration significantly exceeded by both Burnett and Washburn Counties (U.S. Decennial Census 2000a). In fact, the U.S. Department of Agriculture (USDA) Economic Research Service (2004) classified both counties as "retirement destination counties." This indicated that they "experienced 15 percent or more in-migration of people age 60 and older in the 1980s" (USDA 2004). As a group, nonmetropolitan retirement destination counties have experienced much higher population growth than other nonmetropolitan counties as well as high job growth, although frequently in low-paying sectors (USDA 2004). Both counties reflected the racial composition of Wisconsin generally, with very small minority populations (U.S. Decennial Census 2000a).

TABLE 4.3. Study area population characteristics

County	Population	Median age (years)	Percentage of population over 65 years	Percentage of population that is white	Percentage of population that is Hispanic
Burnett	15,674	44.1	20	93	0.80
Washburn	16,036	42.1	19	97	0.90

SOURCE: U.S. Census Bureau 2000a.

Washburn County is a rural county: 83 percent of its population was classified as rural overall, with the city of Spooner being the only county subdivision whose population is less than 90 percent rural.[2] Within the county, there are four subdivisions with seasonal housing levels of less than 10 percent and four subdivisions with concentrations of over 50 percent (U.S. Decennial Census 2000a).

Burnett County is home to even higher levels of seasonal and recreational housing than neighboring Washburn County. By 1990, already nearly 50 percent of these housing units were for seasonal or recreational use, declining slightly to just over 45 percent by 2000 (U.S. Decennial Census 2000a). Burnett County is also more rural than Washburn, with a population classified as 100 percent rural overall and within each county subdivision. This high level of seasonal housing in highly rural Burnett County reflects the patterns of seasonal housing across the United States. Within the county, only two subdivisions reported concentrations of seasonal housing less than 10 percent, and eight subdivisions had levels in excess of 50 percent (U.S. Decennial Census 2000a).

Both counties have higher levels of home ownership than nationwide rates, but this is typical of nonmetropolitan counties in which housing is more affordable and rental markets are less available than urban areas (Bostic and Surette 2001). Although the median housing value in the study area was just slightly over $85,000 (U.S. Decennial Census 2000b), the presence

2. We use the term *subdivision* as defined by the U.S. Census Bureau. Census county subdivisions are small areas of counties that were delineated by the Census Bureau for purposes of presenting statistical data. Subdivisions refer to politically incorporated areas such as towns but may also be a clearly delineated area that is not politically defined, such as unincorporated communities (U.S. Census Bureau 2000d).

of several homes in each county valued at over one million dollars demonstrates the stratification of local housing markets. Fears of increasing property values and subsequent taxes are a central concern of recreation and seasonal housing areas. The high percentage of housing units built since 1970 also demonstrates the significance of recent development in the area (see table 4.4).

Just as there is stratification in the housing market in our study area, there is also income stratification. Both Burnett and Washburn Counties had 5 percent of their population reporting household incomes over $100,000 or approximately three times the median household income (U.S. Decennial Census 2000b). Over 20 percent of each county's households received some form of retirement income in 1999, again confirming the importance of their role as retirement destinations. Each county also had a significant percentage of its population living below the poverty line (see table 4.5). Relatively high levels of job growth and increasing property values in the region have not eradicated the poverty in the area. It should be noted that income measures drawn from the 2000 census do not reflect the income of seasonal residents, who typically report much higher incomes than local residents. We discuss the disparities between seasonal and permanent residents in the next chapter.

Both Burnett and Washburn Counties continue to have a significant level of manufacturing employment, more than twice the national manufacturing employment rate (U.S. Decennial Census 2000b). Although Burnett County did not have information or finance as top employers, these were the fastest-growing sectors of the economy between 2001 and 2005 (U.S. Census Bureau 2005, Burnett County), revealing the high growth in property development and its associated sectors. Similarly, in Washburn

TABLE 4.4. Study area housing characteristics

County	Percentage of housing units built since 1970	Percentage of homes valued at over $200,000	Homes valued at over $1,000,000	Median housing value	Percentage of housing units that are owner occupied	Percentage of housing units that are seasonal
Burnett	60	4	7	$87,500	85	45
Washburn	54	5	10	$85,700	81	35

SOURCE: U.S. Census Bureau 2000b.

TABLE 4.5. Study area economic characteristics

County	Mean travel time to work (minutes)	Percentage of households with income over $100,000	Median household income	Percentage of households with retirement income	Percentage of population below poverty line
Burnett	26.8	5	$34,218	22	9
Washburn	22.4	5	$33,716	21	10

SOURCE: U.S. Census Bureau 2000b.

County, the highest growth during the same period was in professional and technical employment, although this is not a large employer in absolute numbers (U.S. Census Bureau 2005, Washburn County). Accommodations, food services, and retail trade were the largest employment categories in both counties (USDA 2004). The complete absence of extractive employment in the study area reflects the decline of forestry and agriculture in the Pine Barrens. Seasonal residents are a large part of the economic shift of Pine Barrens communities. During interviews in 2009, one local real estate agent said about seasonal residents: "Our service sector could not survive without the seasonal home owner and tourists. We could not live without them. They provide stability for our businesses." A local contractor said: "Construction and home repair businesses do well when the seasonal homeowners are here. We are heavily dependent on seasonal homeowners in our business."

Conclusion

In this chapter we continued our discussion of population and housing growth in rural natural amenity regions, focusing specifically on our study area of northwestern Wisconsin. We also demonstrated that the rise of a new service economy in the upper rural Midwest as a consumption landscape based on the natural amenity features of the region has replaced the earlier production landscape. Pine Barrens communities have shifted their employment base away from the traditional extractive industries of timber and agriculture and toward service industries, construction, and new manufacturing. The rural communities of Wisconsin's Pine Barrens have seen a significant in-migration of new residents, many from urban areas, substantial growth in seasonal housing and housing density, and a conversion of their economies toward recreation development. These changes are altering the composition of the Pine Barrens and placing these natural amenity-rich communities under new and different stresses as they attempt to integrate a diverse population into their communities. In the next three chapters we further narrow our focus to examine community attachment, social networks, community participation, and natural resource values of both seasonal and permanent residents in our Pine Barrens study area.

chapter 5

Community Attachment
Time Heals All Wounds

The community feeling is gone. . . . They've killed the spirit. . . . With
development, there are constantly builders in the area . . . it gets a bit
much . . . I feel like I don't belong here. . . . This is not development.
From the residents' point of view, it is decay, not renewal. It used to
be a village, [now] I don't have many neighbors.

—Resident quoted in G. Visser,
  "Second Homes and Local Development"

IN THE PREVIOUS CHAPTERS we introduced the changes that are
taking place in rural communities on national and regional scales, setting the context for our closer examination of Burnett and Washburn
Counties. In this and the following chapters we begin the third level of our
three-tier analysis: a close examination of how new and seasonal residents
fit into Northwoods communities using data collected by our Natural
Resources and Community Survey (see Clendenning 2004 and appendix C
for more information on the survey). Are seasonal homeowners engaged
in their rural host communities? In what ways? Do they have meaningful
personal relationships with their neighbors? Do newcomers conflict with
long-time residents? We address these questions in the following chapters
by exploring the social aspects of transformation to a consumption landscape and explore the crucial role that time plays in developing community
relationships. The difference between permanent and seasonal residents
is ultimately defined by time: the amount of time spent at a home. Time
determines who is a long-term resident and who is a newcomer, and we find
that time, measured by the number of days spent at their recreational home,
also influences the community attachment of seasonal residents.

WHO ARE THE RESIDENTS?

Before examining the results of our analysis, this section reintroduces the Natural Resources and Community Survey and its sample of residents. During June and July of 2002 we sent the survey to 422 permanent residents and 378 seasonal residents in Burnett and Washburn Counties and received responses from 356 permanent residents and 323 seasonal residents. We are confident that this random sample of homeowners in the two counties accurately represents their communities.[1] There are, however, important differences between the seasonal and permanent residents in our sample, summarized in table 5.1. Permanent residents are an average of three years older than seasonal residents and are slightly more likely to be retired than seasonal residents. They also have fewer children in the home than seasonal residents. Most significant, however, are the substantial differences in education and income between seasonal and permanent residents. The mean income of seasonal residents is approximately $73,000, more than twice the mean income of permanent residents. Seasonal residents also have higher levels of education, with an average educational attainment of a two-year degree. Only five seasonal residents have less than a high school degree in contrast to thirty-three of the permanent residents. Permanent residents have lived in their home for an average of five years longer than seasonal residents. These differences are not unique to our sample and are generally representative of those discussed in other studies of seasonal homeownership (Green and Clendenning 2003; Green et al. 1996; Gustafson 2002; Marcouiller et al. 1996). Later we discuss whether or not these differences are having a major impact on the social landscape of these communities.

Recognizing the differences between permanent and seasonal residents introduced above, let's examine seasonal residents more carefully (see table 5.2). The large majority of seasonal homes are lakefront property, compared to only 30 percent of permanent homes that are on lakefronts. Most seasonal homes were purchased from nonfamily members, although nearly 20 percent were either bought or inherited from family members. On average, seasonal residents spend just over ten weeks at their vacation homes each year, a considerable amount of time. Prior to owning their current home seasonal residents had a variety of experiences in their communities, and only 18 percent bought their homes with no prior experiences. Most seasonal residents have visited the area before, one-quarter of them have

1. See appendix C for a more detailed discussion of survey administration and representativeness.

TABLE 5.1. Basic characteristics of seasonal and permanent homeowners

	Permanent residents			Seasonal residents			Difference	t-value
	N	Mean	SD	N	Mean	SD		
Age	332	58 years	14.15	308	55 years	12.14	3 years	2.440*
Gender	103(f) 227(m)			77(f) 236(m)				-1.869
Income[a]	309	~$32,000 (3.63)	1.67	277	~$73,000 (5.73)	1.61	$41,000 (2.107)	14.712*
Education[b]	332	~some college (3.12)	1.47	313	~2-year degree (4.05)	1.42	~1 year of college (0.928)	-8.120*
Tenure in home	331	24 years	18.05	314	19 years	14.62	5 years	3.846*
No. retired	155			100			55	3.864*
No. of children in home	324	0.364	0.80	302	0.613	1.11	0.248	-3.181

SOURCE: Community and Natural Resources Survey 2002.

[a] Income: 1 = less than $15,000; 2 = $15,000–$24,999; 3 = $25,000–$34,999; 4 = $35,000–$49,999; 5 = $50,000–$74,999; 6 = $75,000–$99,999; 7 = $100,000–$150,000; 8 = $150,000 or more.

[b] Education: 1 = less than high school diploma; 2 = high school diploma or GED; 3 = some college; 4 = 2-year technical or associate degree; 5 = 4-year college degree; 6 = advanced degree.

* $p \leq .05$

TABLE 5.2. Detailed characteristics of seasonal homeowners

Waterfront property	Lake	71%
	River	5%
	None	23%
Acquire home	Purchase from nonfamily	80%
	Purchase from family	9%
	Inherit	8%
Days at home	Mean	72 days
Prior experiences	None	18%
	Owned recreation home	23%
	Rented recreation home	37%
	Visited friends/relatives	17%
	Vacationed	2%
	Resided	0.30%
Plan to move permanently	Within 5 years	25%
	After 5 years	47%

SOURCE: Community and Natural Resources Survey 2002.

previously owned another recreational home in the area, and more than one-third of them had rented a home in the area before. Some are retirees who first vacationed in the area on their honeymoons and grandparents who brought their families for vacations and then decided to buy a home. It is also significant that 47 percent of seasonal homeowners indicate that they are "likely" or "very likely" to move into their vacation homes permanently after five years, and 25 percent agree that this is likely within five years. Conversely, 16 percent of the permanent residents used to be seasonal residents. One real estate broker shared her personal business experiences that confirmed these residential patterns: "Many of my customers have vacationed here with a friend and then later purchase a property. I find this connection is more common than new homeowners returning who have grown up here. . . . Most of the retirees have cabined or vacationed here before moving to the community permanently." So, while seasonal residents in our study do have some important differences from their permanent neighbors, many of them have family connections in the area, have a history of experiences with their communities, and plan to have a long-term connection to their homes and communities.

Interactional Community Theory

Now that we have introduced the seasonal residents of Burnett and Washburn Counties, we ask: are new residents attached to their new homes and communities? Do they feel accepted and supported by their community? What helps new residents to be more attached to their communities? Using the interactional theory of community (Wilkinson 1979, 1991), we focus on the human community and relationships that have been transformed by recreation and natural amenity-led development.

Interactional theory defines relationships and social contact as the true meaning of community; a community is fundamentally a network of social ties and interpersonal interactions. From the interactional approach, communities are fluid and dynamic entities, constantly in flux, and "the local community becomes more dynamic and, perhaps, unstable as a result of the appearance of new actors, new roles, and new arenas of community action" (Wilkinson 1991, 18). However, these changes do not necessarily imply the destruction or loss of community. Instead, interactional scholars continue to assert the fundamental importance of a local community as the primary way in which individuals interact with society.

We developed the Natural Resources and Community Survey with this dynamic definition and understanding of community, and we apply Wilkinson's theory to the analysis within this and the following chapters. The local community remains a primary social structure of daily life and is therefore worthy of continued study. As the structures of rural American communities change to incorporate recreational development and increasingly high levels of seasonal housing in a consumption landscape, questions arise about the present and future well-being of communities of Wisconsin's Northwoods.

By uniting this established conception of community with questions raised by studies of seasonal residents and recreational development, we analyze the impacts of seasonal housing on community well-being. Community well-being has a variety of important implications for the ability of communities to act collectively to protect the fragile social and environmental worlds in which natural amenity-rich rural places exist. Based upon the interactive model of community proposed by Wilkinson, three components of community well-being were measured by our survey: community attachment, local social involvement, and community participation. This chapter presents findings on the community attachment of survey respondents.

Community Engagement of Seasonal Residents

Previous research on seasonal residents has often suggested that seasonal residents are socially isolated from their host communities, forming a community distinct from that of permanent residents (Allen et al. 1988; Girard and Gartner 1993; Jordan 1980). The lives and experiences of seasonal residents are expected to be "clearly separate from the rural milieu within which it is set" (Halseth 1998, 20). The older literature suggests that seasonal residents have few, if any, social ties in the community, little attachment to the host community as a social setting, and little, if any, social cohesion and solidarity with permanent residents. Because seasonal homeowners are often theorized as tourists, their experiences are considered to be shallow and unauthentic. Further, seasonal homeowners are thought to represent a distinct and separate urban culture in their rural host communities, with values, attitudes, beliefs, and collective interests very different from rural residents (see Cuba 1989; Halseth 1998; Hay 1998; Jaakson 1986; Jordan 1980; Tuan 1977). Some new studies have questioned this presumed social distance between seasonal homeowners and their host communities. Many scholars have found that a desire for community can be an important motivation behind seeking second-home ownership (Shellito 2006; Stewart and Stynes 2006) and that seasonal residents establish real, meaningful, and substantive relationships with their second-home communities. If earlier critics were correct, we would expect to see that seasonal residents have very low levels of community attachment, with high income and education having a very negative impact on community attachment. If more recent optimists were correct, we would expect seasonal residents to have positive levels of community attachment and to see less of a difference between the community attachment of seasonal and permanent residents. We explore these relationships as they exist in the unique context of northwestern Wisconsin and find that seasonal homeowners have a more nuanced relationship with their host communities than previously theorized, largely influenced by the amount of time spent at their seasonal homes.

ATTITUDES TOWARD COMMUNITY PARTICIPATION

First, we examine permanent and seasonal residents' attitudes about participating in community affairs. We asked residents how they felt about participating in the community and who should be participating in the community, and we found several significant differences between seasonal and permanent residents (see table 5.3). Both permanent and seasonal residents

TABLE 5.3. Attitudes toward community affairs

	Permanent			Seasonal				
	N	Mean	SD	N	Mean	SD	Difference	t-value
I am interested in community affairs[a]	328	4.33	0.89	315	4.35	0.04	0.01	0.22
I feel welcome participating in the community[b]	324	3.46	1.12	306	2.76	1.00	0.70	−8.25***
I feel that my views are considered fairly when I participate in the community	324	3.23	1.13	305	2.73	1.00	0.51	−5.94***
I feel that my input will not make a difference when I participate in the community	323	3.16	1.17	308	3.36	1.08	0.20	2.18*
I feel that the input of seasonal homeowners is important in community affairs	323	3.50	1.16	310	4.08	1.10	0.58	6.47***
I feel that seasonal homeowners should not participate in community affairs	326	2.68	1.33	310	1.72	0.98	−0.96	−10.30***

SOURCE: Community and Natural Resources Survey 2002.

[a] 5 = very interested; 4 = moderately interested; 3 = neither interested nor disinterested; 2 = moderately disinterested; 1 = very disinterested.
[b] 5 = strongly agree; 4 = somewhat agree; 3 = neither agree nor disagree; 2 = somewhat disagree; 1 = strongly disagree.
*p ≤ .05; **p ≤ .01; ***p ≤ .001

agree that they are interested in community affairs, broadly defined. There was no significant difference between the desires of permanent and seasonal residents to be involved in their communities—both groups want to participate.

When asked about who *should* participate in the community and the *impacts* of participation, however, there are clear differences in attitudes between year-round and seasonal residents. Seasonal residents reported that they felt less welcome participating in their communities than permanent residents. Seasonal residents do not feel completely welcome participating in community decisions and activities. Seasonal residents are also less likely to believe that their views are considered fairly in community decisions. Part-time residents may feel that their neighbors dismiss their opinions and that their contributions are not respected. This feeling of being unwelcome or a lack of acceptance from permanent residents may discourage seasonal residents from fully engaging with their host communities. However, it is permanent residents who think that their input will have less of an actual impact on community decisions. Permanent residents feel more welcome to participate in community affairs, but when decisions are made they feel disempowered and believe they cannot make a difference.

Next we explore our respondents' specific attitudes toward participation of seasonal residents. Permanent residents are less likely to agree that the input of seasonal residents is important to community affairs. Their responses suggest permanent residents have an attitude that their communities do not need the participation of seasonal residents. In contrast to seasonal residents, permanent residents more often agree with the statement that seasonal residents *should not* participate in community affairs. In fact, 28 percent of permanent residents agree that seasonal residents should not participate in community affairs. While this is a minority of year-round residents, a substantial proportion of the community believe that seasonal residents have no place participating in or contributing to community decisions. Clearly there is some disagreement in the communities of Burnett and Washburn Counties about the appropriate role of seasonal residents and whether they have anything to offer their host communities.

Community Attachment

The next aspect of community engagement we examine is community attachment. Community and place attachment have recently garnered a lot of attention in rural sociological studies (see Stedman 2002 for review) and are meant to represent individuals' emotional ties to a place or community. The measures of community attachment selected for this study were based on measures used by Clendenning and Field (2005) to analyze individual-level community engagement and focus on attachment to the human community of the area rather than the physical place. This reflects our use of an interactional definition of *community attachment*, distinct from measures of *place attachment* that emphasize attachment to natural resources or physical surroundings (see Stedman 2003, for example).

To measure community attachment, respondents were asked to answer the following questions using a five-point scale (strongly agree = 5, somewhat agree = 4, neither agree nor disagree = 3, disagree = 2, strongly disagree = 1):

1. The more time I spend in this community, the more I feel I belong.
2. I feel I am fully accepted as a member of this community.
3. If I was in trouble, most people in this community would go out of their way to help me.
4. Most people in this community can be trusted.

Differences between Seasonal and Permanent Residents

Our results indicate that permanent residents have significantly higher levels of community attachment than seasonal homeowners (see table 5.4). However, although seasonal homeowners have significantly lower levels of community attachment, all measures of attachment are positive, suggesting that seasonal homeowners have developed meaningful attachments to the communities where they own their homes. Seasonal homeowners are attached to their communities and have developed relationships of trust with their neighbors. The one area in which seasonal residents demonstrate the largest distance from permanent residents is in their feelings of acceptance. Seasonal homeowners agree that they feel they belong, that they could count on others to help in an emergency, and that they can trust members of their community. In contrast, they are slightly ambivalent when asked if they are fully accepted members of the community. This may reflect a feeling of perceived discrimination or being unwelcome by their neighbors. The lower agreement with a feeling of acceptance mirrors some of the social tensions highlighted by critics such as Jaakson (1986), who believes that animosity and tension between seasonal and permanent residents is inevitable, but the lack of acceptance was felt by the seasonal residents, rather than by permanent

TABLE 5.4. Respondents' levels of community attachment

	Permanent residents			Seasonal homeowners				
	N	Mean	SD	n	Mean	SD	t-value	p-value
Feel I belong here[a]	336	4.24	1.05	317	3.91	1.02	−5.07	< .0001
Feel fully accepted	336	4.24	1.08	317	3.33	1.16	−12.58	< .0001
People would help	336	4.16	1.06	317	3.73	1.06	−6.48	< .0001
People can be trusted	336	4.06	1.06	317	3.74	0.97	−4.98	< .0001
Community attachment[b]	331	16.96	2.97	315	14.81	3.17	8.88	< .0001

SOURCE: Community and Natural Resources Survey 2002.

[a] 5 = strongly agree; 4 = somewhat agree; 3 = neither agree nor disagree; 2 = disagree; 1 = strongly disagree.

[b] Responses to the first four questions were later combined into a single additive scale to represent the degree of community attachment. This additive scale for measuring community attachment was modeled after similar scales used by Clendenning and Field (2005), M. Smith, Krannich, and Hunter (2001), and Krannich and Greider (1984).

residents. This contrasts with the loss of community identity and acceptance felt by longtime permanent residents described by scholars such as Halseth (1998). Halseth's ethnography of rural "cottage country" in Canada argues that permanent residents are losing their feelings of connection and attachment to their community because they feel that seasonal residents have changed their communities to fit their own ideals. This does not seem to be the case for permanent residents of the Pine Barrens, who instead respond with higher levels of community attachment than their seasonal counterparts. Seasonal residents clearly demonstrate lower levels of community attachment than permanent residents, but they report a lot of positive community attachment, supporting other works that have found second-home owners do have significant attachments to their host communities.

CREATING COMMUNITY ATTACHMENT

Given that seasonal residents have lower levels of community attachment, what specific traits might explain this difference? Is it because seasonal residents are wealthier than their neighbors, as suggested by Salamon (2003)? Or perhaps higher levels of education isolate seasonal residents from rural communities. Maybe they just haven't been in Pine Barrens communities long enough to establish attachment. By creating a single scale to represent community attachment, we are able to measure the impacts of these different factors on the overall level of community attachment. We built statistical models to determine the relative importance of several variables for predicting levels of attachment for both seasonal and permanent residents.[2] This allows us to examine several variables at once and isolate the effects of each while controlling the others. For example, with proper modeling, we can determine whether people's community attachment is higher with high

---

2. In order to perform the Ordinary Least Squares regressions soundly, we transformed the dependent variable to increase normality. Because the variable was very heavily right-skewed, we utilized a square-root transformation, which greatly increased the normality of both the variable and the residuals of the full models. Outliers were also removed based on analysis of the studentized residuals including the Cook's D statistic of each outlier point. To create a reduced model we ran step-wise forward (significance level of $p = .2$ to enter the model) and backward regression (significance level of $p = .2$ to remain in the model). In general, each selection procedure identified identical significant variables. When the forward and backward regression procedures did not retain identical variables, we kept all of the variables identified by each. We then reanalyzed the data with the reduced number of independent variables.

incomes or lower with high incomes, regardless of their education. This modeling allows us to explain different levels of community attachment for both seasonal and permanent residents, expanding existing theories of rural community that examine community-level changes (see Johnson and Beale 2002) or offer only limited explanation of differences in community attachment.

The first analysis included the full sample of both groups of residents, while the latter two separated the subpopulations to examine differences between them. In the first analysis, both seasonal and permanent resident responses were included, in contrast to most existing studies that separate the populations. In their study of second homes in northern Wisconsin and Minnesota, Marcouiller et al. (1996) used this holistic approach in order to provide insights into both groups. In this case, we decided to include both groups because of our theoretical concern with the community in its entirety, including both seasonal and permanent residents, and a focus on the interaction between both groups. This full model included eleven independent measures: five social indicators and six demographic indicators.

Based on the differences between seasonal and permanent residents that we outlined above as well as previous studies on seasonal residency, we selected eleven measures to analyze. Each of the following eleven measures tells a story about how the social landscapes of Northwoods communities are being transformed:

1. Seasonal versus permanent residency
2. How long someone has lived in the community
3. Whether their property is waterfront
4. If they spent their childhood in a rural area
5. Whether they have children in the home
6. Age
7. Age-squared[3]
8. Education
9. Income
10. Gender
11. Whether they are retired

3. For an explanation of age-squared as well as other details on how the models were constructed and analyzed, see appendix A.

For each of these measures we ask the question, does this significantly affect someone's community attachment?

Length of residence has consistently been found to be the strongest predictor of community attachment (Fischer et al. 1977; Goudy 1982, 1990; Hummon 1992; Kasarda and Janowitz 1974; Sampson 1988). In addition, higher levels of education and income, the age of the residents, and the presence of children are often associated with higher levels of community attachment (Fischer 1982, 1984; Hummon 1992; Hunter 1975, 1978; Kasarda and Janowitz 1974; Sampson 1988). Higher levels of education and income are associated with more community participation, but both are often associated with fewer local social ties. Fischer et al. (1977) suggest that this is because wealthier, better-educated individuals have more resources with which they are able to retain strong social ties with distant friends and family, and therefore they make fewer connections in their local communities. Older people often have higher levels of community participation but lower numbers of family and friendship ties, while presence of children is associated with higher levels of community participation and local social ties (Fischer et al. 1977; Hummon 1992; Hunter 1974; Kasarda and Janowitz 1974; Sampson 1988). Local social ties and community participation are in turn associated with community attachment. As Kasarda and Janowitz (1974) argue, the establishment of friendship and family ties as well as local organization ties has the effect of strengthening community attachment.

SEASONAL RESIDENTS

But what about seasonal homeowners specifically? While there are many studies of community attachment and participation for permanent residents, we also wanted to look at seasonal residents to see if they had a different story to tell. Very few studies look closely at seasonal homeowners to see what influences their involvement in their host communities. To do this we ran a separate statistical model (OLS regression model) that only included seasonal residents. In addition to the eleven measures listed above, three more were included in the seasonal residents' analysis: number of days spent at the seasonal home, an intention of migrating to the community, and previous residence in the community.[4] The number of days spent at a

4. The independent variable for intention to relocate was created from the two survey questions asking people if they intended to relocate to the area within five years or after five years. Any respondent who reported "very likely" to either question received a positive score in this new dummy variable for intention to relocate.

seasonal home has been found by Kaltenborn (1997) to be significantly associated with sense of place. It is quite possible that the amount of time spent at the seasonal home, rather than the number of years of ownership, has a larger impact on community attachment, social ties, and community participation. The likelihood of migrating was used because we found that substantial proportions of the seasonal homeowners intend to retire to their seasonal residence or make it their full-time residence before retirement. This is similar to Bill Freudenburg's (1986) notion of anticipated length of residence. Freudenburg (1986) argues that a person who expects to reside in a community for a long period of time has more incentive to develop social ties than someone who expects to leave the community. Our findings suggest that seasonal homeowners who intend to move to their seasonal home on a full-time basis are more likely to develop social ties, become involved in community affairs, and feel more attached to the community. Further, we expect that seasonal homeowners who previously lived in the community have higher levels of attachment, more extensive social ties, and participate more in community activities.

Discussion

Overall, we were not able to predict very much of the variation of community attachment (see appendix A). Community attachment is a complex social process, and these eleven variables do not offer a complete explanation of how people develop attachments to their communities. What these analyses do, however, is allow us to compare the *relative* importance of different traits in shaping someone's community attachment. Beginning with the analysis of the combined population of both seasonal and permanent residents, our findings demonstrate a persistent, negative impact of seasonal resident status. This means that regardless of other social and demographic variables such as high income and urban background, seasonal residents still reported significantly lower levels of community attachment than permanent residents.[5] The negative effect of seasonal homeownership on community attachment, then, seems to be something inherent, even without the other social and demographic factors at hand. This is not to say that these

5. None of the other independent variables approach the explanatory power of seasonal residency, although the very small effect of age-squared indicates that the community attachment of adults did increase in late life stages after generally declining throughout most life stages.

social and demographic characteristics have no impact on how attached people are to their communities (several of them do have small impacts), but they do not completely explain the lower levels of community attachment reported by seasonal residents.[6] This indicates a substantial need for further research in order to isolate some of the social, demographic, cultural, and psychological factors that are important influences on community attachment.

Looking at the analysis for only permanent residents, our findings resemble the findings of many traditional community studies because of the significance of duration of residence and life stage (represented by age-squared). Confirming the findings of many traditional community scholars, long-term residency significantly increases the level of community attachment for permanent residents (see appendix A). Permanent residents who have lived in an area for more than ten years have significantly higher levels of community attachment than their counterparts. This effect was found in neither the combined community model nor that for seasonal residents. The continued significance of the age-squared term again indicates the increase in community attachment demonstrated by much older adults.

In the analysis that included only seasonal residents, the total number of days spent at the seasonal home and the likelihood of migration were the only significant predictors of community attachment. The number of days spent at the home was positively related to community attachment, demonstrating that residents who spent more time at their seasonal home throughout the year felt more attached to their community and neighbors than their peers.[7] This mirrors similar findings by Stedman (2008) in which

6. The very poor fit of the analysis generally, represented by the low R-squared value, however, indicates that these variables based on previous studies actually explain very little about how community members establish community attachments in our study area. A higher R-squared value would mean that these eleven factors together explain what makes people more or less attached to their communities. Instead, our R-squared value is quite low, which means that there are other important factors of community attachment not accounted for with these eleven measures.

7. Both the number of days spent visiting during fall and the number of days spent visiting during summer significantly increased the attachment of seasonal residents, while winter and spring days did not. The relationship was more than twice as strong for the fall days as for the summer days and more than four times that of total days. This indicates that residents who visit during the off-season months of the fall reported substantially higher levels of attachment to their host community.

the amount of time spent visiting the home was shown to be an important factor driving community and place attachment. This argues for a new conceptualization of seasonal or permanent residency as a continuum rather than a binary (either/or) measure. As seasonal homeowners spend more time in their host communities, they move farther on the continuum toward permanent residency. Importantly, the inverse could also be true: seasonal homeowners who are more attached to their community may choose to spend more days visiting the home. Our model does not allow us to determine the direction of causality, but the relationship between time spent at the seasonal home and increased community attachment is clear. Importantly, in contrast to the expectations raised by newcomer/old-timer conflict literature, the long-term residency of seasonal residents had no impact on their attachment to the host community. Seasonal residents who expected to relocate to the area permanently had significantly higher levels of community attachment than their peers. This demonstrates that those residents who planned to migrate were already establishing important emotional ties to their community and neighbors, preparing for a permanent entry.[8] Demographic characteristics were insignificant, demonstrating no effect on the community attachment of seasonal residents (see appendix A). Again, this is in contrast to the explanations of many newcomer/old-timer studies and early second-home studies in which it was assumed that the generally higher levels of education and income and the age of seasonal homeowners created social distance and friction with host communities (Hay 1998; Jaakson 1986; Jordan 1980; Tuan 1977). Although the model for seasonal residents left much of the variance in community attachment unexplained, the larger R-squared value for the seasonal model indicates the importance of the number of visiting days and an intention to relocate to the area. We are better at explaining why seasonal homeowners are attached to their communities than we were at explaining the community attachment of permanent homeowners. The significance of the number of visiting days and an intention to relocate indicates that together these two features offered our best explanation of the community attachment of seasonal residents.

8. Again, the inverse could also be true: those seasonal residents with strong ties and connections to the community may be more likely to want to relocate to the area permanently.

SUMMARY

What is apparent from this first examination of seasonal homeowners and their permanent counterparts is that seasonal residents have very different relationships with their communities than their permanent neighbors. Seasonal and permanent residents disagree about whether seasonal residents should be involved in their communities and whose opinions are valued in community decisions. Seasonal residents don't feel entirely welcome participating in their communities, and 28 percent of permanent residents believe that seasonal residents should not participate at all in community affairs. Regarding community attachment, the variables that other scholars have found important in shaping the community attachment of rural and urban residents (social status, age, and length of residence) do not affect the community engagement of seasonal residents.[9] Seasonal residents are less attached to their host communities than their permanent neighbors, but this does not appear to be due to higher incomes or education creating social distance. Instead, the results seem to indicate that there is something inherent in seasonal homeownership that inhibits community attachment. Are seasonal homeowners less attached to their host communities because they do not have many friends in the area? Is it because they are less involved in the daily activities of the community? We explore these questions further in the next chapter, examining friendship and family ties and community involvement of residents.

Permanent residents' community attachment, in contrast, is significantly related to both their length of residence and life stage (represented by age-squared), in line with the findings of many systemic community scholars. While seasonal residents' community attachment does not seem to be explained by the traditional variables of previous community studies, the number of days they spend at their seasonal home annually and an intention to make the home a permanent residence do significantly increase their reported attachment. We believe that these measures of seasonal residents' current and expected presence in their host community are best understood as very similar to length of residence for permanent residents. Length of residence, current visiting habits, and expected future residence are variables that can provide seasonal residents with the opportunity and motivation

9. This substantive interpretation of the lack of effects for demographic characteristics must be taken with caution, however, as the actual distribution of income, education, and age for seasonal residents is fairly small.

to engage with their communities. Our understanding of community can be expanded to address seasonal residents if annual visitation time and intention to migrate are recognized as serving the same role in supporting community attachment as long-term residency does for permanent residents.

CONCLUSION

In the previous chapters, we have described the population change taking place in many rural natural amenity regions and in northern Wisconsin in particular as the regions shift from production to consumption landscapes. We have noted the distinctive features and character of new in-migrants to Wisconsin's Pine Barrens. In a similar fashion we have noted the significant imprint seasonal residency and seasonal housing are leaving on the social organization of community and the social environment of communities. Community attachment is one part of the human landscape of a community, and seasonal homeowners' lower level of community attachment is altering the social fabric of Northwoods communities. We find some evidence of social unrest around seasonal residents, as they do not feel entirely accepted and welcome within their host communities. Importantly, we are also starting to understand that there is a subgroup of seasonal residents who are very attached to their new communities and who spend many more days there each year or hope to make their home a permanent home. One such closely attached seasonal resident shared her positive feelings about the Pine Barrens community: "Do we feel welcome here? Of course! We certainly feel accepted by local residents and often host or are hosted at weekend gatherings where both summer residents like us and [permanent residents] participate." Clearly, frequent interaction with her neighbors is an important part of why she feels welcome in the community. In the next chapter we explore these interactions. What about the friendship and family ties of seasonal residents? Do they integrate into the community through friendship and neighbor relationships with permanent residents? In what community activities and affairs are seasonal residents involved? We continue our exploration of the impacts of seasonal homeownership on Pine Barrens communities in the next chapter.

chapter 6

Local Social Ties and Community Participation

Time Heals All Wounds

Remember, you're *not* a tourist.

—Wisconsin Seasonal Residents Association, Inc.

IN THE PREVIOUS CHAPTER we introduced the residents in our study and examined the community attachment of seasonal and permanent residents. We found that seasonal residents do indeed report lower levels of attachment to their host communities. However, those who reported spending more time in their seasonal community or who planned to make a permanent move to their seasonal home had higher levels of attachment than their peers. We began to see that seasonal residency is a complex phenomena and that seasonal residents are not a homogenous group. In this chapter we delve further into the relationship of seasonal residents to their host communities by looking at their social networks with friends, families, and neighbors and their reported participation in important community events.

The interactional understanding of community (Wilkinson 1991) that we introduced in chapter 5 emphasizes the importance of interpersonal ties and social interactions in creating and sustaining community. According to Wilkinson, nothing is more important to a community than ordinary, consistent interaction with your neighbors. The ability of seasonal homeowners to establish social ties and engage in different forms of community participation is unclear, however. How involved are seasonal residents in their communities? What levels and types of participation are common? We delve into these questions by exploring the local social ties and community participation of seasonal residents. The first section of this chapter describes the similarities and differences of local family and friendship ties of permanent and seasonal residents and the important factors shaping those social ties. In particular, we look at friendship, family, and neighbor relationships that cross the gap between seasonal and permanent residents. The second section of the chapter contrasts the different types of community participation of seasonal and permanent residents.

LOCAL SOCIAL TIES

As Pine Barrens communities experience a shift toward recreation and natural amenity-based development and subsequently increase the significance of seasonal residency to their communities, the social organization of those communities is transformed. While community attachment represents one important aspect of community change introduced by seasonal residents, the extent and type of friendship, family, and neighbor ties represent an equally important type of transformation. If seasonal homeowners exhibit lower levels of friendship and family ties than permanent residents, or if they are socially isolated from their permanent neighbors, this would have important implications for the health of Pine Barrens communities. Drawing from Wilkinson's interactional understanding of community, this section examines the extent of seasonal residents' social networks as well as the depth of cross-group ties between seasonal and permanent residents. We begin with a description of the social networks presented through the survey and then proceed into statistical analysis to examine how these social networks are shaped.

First, we compared the numbers of social ties of each type of resident. Our survey asked residents to estimate approximately how many close personal adult friends and adult relatives they had in their community or within a one-hour drive. According to interactional theory, higher numbers of close friends and family in the local community support strong community cohesion and identity, and these basic numbers help us tell whether residents' important relationships are within their local community. Not surprisingly, permanent residents had more close friends and family in the area than seasonal homeowners (see table 6.1). However, seasonal homeowners also had some local social networks. In fact, nearly 90 percent had at least one close personal friend in the area, and nearly 45 percent had family in the community. The most noticeable difference between seasonal and permanent residents is that not very many seasonal residents had more than a few close friends and family in the area. Fewer than 30 percent of seasonal homeowners had more than ten close friends in the community (whereas nearly 65 percent of permanent residents had more than ten close friends), and

TABLE 6.1. Friendship and family ties by type of resident

| | Permanent | | | Seasonal | | | | |
	n	Mean	SD	n	Mean	SD	t-value	p-value
No. of friends	320	25.25	26.06	309	11.25	15.15	8.27	< .0001
No. of family	327	8.44	14.51	308	2.90	6.53	6.26	< .0001

	n	%	n	%	χ^2	p-value
No. of friends						
0	4	1.25	40	12.99		
1 to 5	46	14.38	83	26.95		
6 to 10	66	20.63	95	30.84		
11 to 20	93	29.06	51	16.56		
over 20	111	34.69	39	12.66	91.9	< .0001

	n	%	n	%	χ^2	p-value
No. of family						
0	82	25.15	171	55.52		
1 to 5	126	38.65	92	29.87		
6 to 10	50	15.34	22	7.14		
11 to 20	34	10.43	15	4.87		
over 20	34	10.43	8	2.60	70.51	< .0001

SOURCE: Community and Natural Resources Survey 2002.

fewer than 15 percent of seasonal homeowners had more than five family ties in the community (while over 36 percent of permanent residents had more than five family ties). So, seasonal residents do have some important social ties to their community, but in comparison to permanent residents their social networks in the area are fairly limited. They may have a few close friends and family in the area, but permanent residents have many more connections and much larger local social networks.

Because many scholars assume seasonal residents are socially isolated from their permanent neighbors (see Cuba and Hummon 1993; Halseth 1998; Hay 1998; Jaakson 1986; Jordan 1980; Tuan 1977), we also examined the social ties between seasonal and permanent residents, focusing on cross-group ties that may bridge the gap between seasonal and permanent residents. Turning to social ties with other type of residents, we see that permanent residents reported fewer friends and family who were seasonal homeowners than vice versa. Seasonal homeowners reported statistically significant larger numbers of friends and family ties that were permanent residents (see table 6.2). It is encouraging for community development to find that seasonal residents are reporting some important relationships with their permanent neighbors and not associating only with other seasonal residents.

Further examining cross-group ties, we found that nearly 70 percent of seasonal homeowners reported at least one friend who was a permanent resident. Seasonal homeowners in the Pine Barrens report that they are not as socially isolated from permanent residents as Halseth (1998) found in his Canadian study areas. Similarly, over 25 percent of seasonal homeowners had family ties to permanent residents. This supports recent findings that local social ties are an important component of second home-ownership (McIntyre 2006). These cross-group ties seem to indicate that seasonal homeowners are making social ties with permanent neighbors or have chosen their second home because of existing social ties in the community. At least in part, these cross group interactions are a necessity for seasonal homeowners—they are still the minority in most communities, and most permanent residents have long-established ties to the area and the local economy. It is noteworthy, however, that seasonal residents do report having some significant relationships with permanent residents, and this holds potential for building healthy communities.

But what about neighbors? We also asked residents to estimate what percentage of their neighbors were permanent and seasonal residents to see whether the groups of residents were living together as neighbors. We find

TABLE 6.2. Social ties with the "other" type of resident

	Permanent			Seasonal			t-value	p-value
	n	Mean	SD	n	Mean	SD		
Mean no. of "other" friends	318	4.01	9.56	308	6.5	16.93	-2.26	0.02
Mean no. of "other" family ties	325	0.52	1.94	304	1.97	5.91	-4.07	< .0001

No. of other friends	n	%		n	%		χ^2	p-value
0	164	51.57		98	31.82			
1 to 5	100	31.45		122	39.61			
6 to 10	29	9.12		47	15.26			
11 to 20	11	3.46		28	9.09			
over 20	14	4.40		13	4.22		30.4	< .0001

No. of other family ties	n	%		n	%		χ^2	p-value
0	270	83.08		223	75.36			
1 to 5	48	14.77		53	17.43			
6 to 10	6	1.85		12	3.95			
over 10	1	0.31		16	5.26		19.3	0.0002

SOURCE: Community and Natural Resources Survey 2002.

that both seasonal and permanent residents do not have many "other" neighbors, but seasonal residents may not be as physically isolated from permanent residents as Halseth (1998) found and as other studies have assumed. In fact, permanent residents were more likely to live in areas that were physically more isolated from seasonal homeowners (see table 6.3). This is at least partially due to the fact that a substantial portion of permanent residents (18 percent) lived in cities and villages while only 2 percent of seasonal homeowners had homes in cities and villages. Thus, 18 percent of permanent residents are essentially geographically isolated from seasonal homeowners because so few seasonal homeowners live within the cities or villages of the Pine Barrens. Also, over 70 percent of seasonal residents owned lakeshore property, while this was true for only 30 percent of permanent residents. This suggests that lakeside neighborhoods where seasonal residents tend to live are not home to many permanent residents. The importance of housing location, particularly lakeside location, was also emphasized in interviews with Pine Barrens residents. One seasonal resident stated: "My main contacts with local [permanent] residents are with those who live on the lake and are part of our [Lake] Association." Another reiterated the importance of lakeside communities: "My community is the Lake Association. Those year-around folks who have lake property or local businesses are our friends." Many Pine Barrens communities, particularly for seasonal residents, revolve around their local lake, and permanent residents simply do not have high rates of lakeshore property ownership. In these natural amenity communities, the concentration of seasonal homes around lakes is

TABLE 6.3. Percentage of neighbors who are "other" type of resident

Percentage of neighbors	Permanent ($n = 311$)		Seasonal ($n = 300$)		χ^2	p-value
	n	%	n	%		
0	95	30.55	40	13.33		
0.1 to 25	92	29.58	99	33.00		
25 to 50	42	13.50	58	19.33		
51 to 75	46	14.79	53	17.67		
over 75	36	11.58	50	16.67	27.81	< .0001

SOURCE: Community and Natural Resources Survey 2002.

both a physical and social barrier to interactions between seasonal and permanent residents.

From these different examinations of social networks we draw a cautiously encouraging message: seasonal homeowners are not socially isolated from permanent residents. In contrast, they actually demonstrated significant, although relatively small, social networks and more cross-group interactions with permanent residents as friends, family, and neighbors than vice versa. Still, the majority of both seasonal and permanent residents have very limited cross-group ties, and these social networks need to be supported in order to draw residents together.

In addition to asking residents about the number of their social ties in the community, we asked them to estimate how *often* they socialized with those friends and family. Not surprisingly, permanent residents socialized more often with each of their social ties (friends, family, and neighbors) than seasonal homeowners. However, a significant group of seasonal homeowners socialized several times a month or more with friends (nearly 50 percent), family (over 40 percent), and neighbors (nearly 35 percent). We also asked community members how often they socialized with the other type of resident, and seasonal homeowners reported more frequent social interaction with permanent residents than vice versa (see table 6.4). This is likely due in part to different base levels of social interaction upon which respondents were drawing. That is, seasonal homeowners visit their homes only occasionally and thus have lower levels of social interaction than permanent residents. Thus a relatively small amount of social interaction may be perceived as "sometimes" or "often." In contrast, permanent residents, on average, have more frequent social interaction with other members of their

TABLE 6.4. Frequency of social interaction with "other" type of resident

	Permanent (*n* = 322)		Seasonal (*n* = 298)			
	n	%	*n*	%	χ^2	*p*-value
Never	51	15.84	18	6.04		
Rarely	71	22.05	64	21.48		
Sometimes	129	40.06	138	46.31		
Often	71	22.05	78	26.17	15.87	0.001

SOURCE: Community and Natural Resources Survey 2002.

home community and may judge the same amount of social interaction with seasonal residents as "rarely" or even "never."

Now that we understand something about the size and type of social networks in the Pine Barrens, we also want to know what factors shape someone's friendship and family ties in their community. Do residents with higher income socialize more often? Do long-term residents have more family ties in the area? Similar to our analysis of community attachment in chapter 5, by examining local social ties using statistical models (logistic and OLS regression), we are able to identify the characteristics that are strongly related to social networks. Again, this modeling allows us to identify some of the factors that explain differences in social networks, moving beyond the simple awareness of those differences.

Previous studies have found several important factors that influence community engagement and social ties, such as the length of residence, income, education, urban residence, and other sociodemographic characteristics. Jordan (1980) and others have speculated that demographic differences between seasonal and permanent residents were responsible for social tensions between the groups and a lack of community engagement (Coppock 1977a; Girard and Gartner 1993; Gustafson 2002; Henshal 1977; Liu and Var 1986; Pizam 1978; Romeril 1984; Sheldon and Var 1984). As in chapter 5, we examine eleven basic social and demographic characteristics for all residents: seasonal or permanent residency, how long they have lived in the community, whether their property is waterfront, whether they spent their childhood in a rural area, whether they have children in the home, their age, age-squared, education, income, gender, and retirement. Three additional variables are examined for seasonal residents: number of days spent at the seasonal home, an intention to migrate to the community, and previous residence in the community.[1] In this section we examine all of these variables to find out if they have any influence on local social ties.

Our analyses note that, like the findings on community attachment, the number of days that seasonal residents spend at their home each year has the most significant impact on their local social ties. The more days that seasonal residents spent in their Pine Barrens homes, the more close friends

1. The independent variable for intention to relocate was created from the two survey questions asking people if they intended to relocate to the area within five years or after five years. Any respondent who reported "very likely" to either question received a positive score in this new dummy variable for intention to relocate.

they had in the area, the more friends they had who were permanent residents, and the more often they socialized with neighbors and permanent residents. Again, this suggests that the simple reality of spending more time in the community each year allows seasonal residents to become more engaged with their neighbors and to bridge the gap with permanent residents, or it indicates that seasonal residents with strong ties in the community choose to spend more time at their homes. Long-term seasonal residents who have lived in the area for more than seven years and those who intend to move to the area permanently are also much more likely to have at least one close friend who is a permanent resident. They have more time and intentions invested in the community and are more likely to have established important relationships with permanent residents. As we found in chapter 5, there seems to be a continuum of seasonal to permanent residency, with seasonal residents who spend a large number of days visiting their second homes or who intend to relocate to the area overcoming some of the social breaks with permanent residents.

The same is true for seasonal residents who have previously resided in the Pine Barrens: they have more close friends and family in the area and are much more likely to have family members who are permanent residents. Seasonal residents who have previously lived in the area are also much more likely to have family ties in their community, suggesting that for some seasonal homeowners the seasonal home represents a link to family and childhood place of residence. For some seasonal homeowners the seasonal home was a part of a migration cycle in which residents had left their childhood homes, but they retained ties to that community and intended to return to their childhood homes, perhaps in retirement. One seasonal resident said during an interview: "I feel like I have lived here all my life. I grew up here, my friends are here, and my husband is from here." The boundaries between seasonal homeowner and permanent resident appear somewhat fluid and ambiguous in the Pine Barrens. Relatedly, we also found that seasonal residents with a rural childhood home are significantly more likely to have a close personal friend who is a permanent resident. Their rural childhood experience seems to bridge some of the cultural gaps between seasonal and permanent residents.

Our analyses also demonstrate the repeated barrier of waterfront property for relationships between seasonal and permanent residents. While having waterfront property had no statistically significant impacts for the social networks of seasonal residents, waterfront property changed the social relationships of permanent residents.[2] Permanent residents who have water-front homes spend much more time socializing than others, and they social-ize with seasonal residents much more often. Again, this supports a more fluid understanding of seasonal and permanent residency in the Pine Bar-rens; these waterfront permanent residents overcome some of the barriers between permanent and seasonal residents.

This analysis offers some optimism about the relationships between sea-sonal and permanent residents. Some seasonal residents have meaningful friendships and family ties with their permanent neighbors and are not socially isolated. Overall, we found again that seasonal residents are not a homogenous group; there are significant differences in the way they engage with their new communities. We did find some small negative effects of high education and income that suggest the isolating effects of these dif-ferences found by Salamon (2003) and others are not entirely absent in Pine Barrens communities. Still, seasonal and permanent residents do have social ties that reach across the groups, particularly for seasonal residents who spend large amounts of time at their second homes or who have previously lived in the area.

COMMUNITY PARTICIPATION

Beyond community attachment and local social ties, another critical meas-ure of community is the extent to which residents participate in community affairs—do residents belong to community groups, participate in public events and meetings, and volunteer their time for community groups? In his theory of interactive community, Wilkinson (1991) emphasizes the impor-tance of casual social ties and connection, but also the community field in which collective action is taken on behalf of the community at large. Mea-sures of community participation are important indicators of local society, the opportunity for interpersonal connections and interactions, and the potential for a community field. We measured community participation using respondents' estimates and responses to the following questions:

1. Number of hours per month spent volunteering with a community organization

2. The lack of impact for seasonal residents is largely due to the lack of variance on this variable; there are not enough seasonal residents who do not have waterfront property for this variable to gain statistical significance.

2. Contacted a public official in the last year (1 = yes, 0 = no)
3. Participation in a community project in the last year (1 = yes, 0 = no)
4. Number of community groups to which respondent belongs
5. Attended a community event in the past year (1 = yes, 0 = no)
6. Attended a community meeting in the past year (1 = yes, 0 = no).

Not surprisingly, permanent residents had significantly higher levels of participation in all measures of community participation than seasonal homeowners except for one: contacting public officials (see table 6.5). Permanent residents belonged to more community groups, volunteered more of their time, and participated in more community activities (except contacting public officials). Membership in community organizations for permanent residents was comparable to results commonly found in national surveys. For example, Putnam (2000) reported that 73 percent of Americans belong to at least one community organization (compared to 62 percent of the permanent residents in this study). However, what was surprising was the extent to which at least a subpopulation of seasonal homeowners was engaged in community affairs. Nearly 45 percent of seasonal homeowners belonged to at least one community group, and nearly 15 percent belonged to two or more community groups. However, the most common community organizations to which seasonal homeowners belong were lake associations (40 percent of seasonal homeowners were members of lake associations). One seasonal resident shared the centrality of their lake association as their main community group: "We spend a lot, a lot, of time with our lake association. We volunteer and we help with fundraisers and plan events. We do not get involved with other community groups during the time we are here." Lake associations address needs and concerns that most directly affect most

TABLE 6.5. Membership in community groups

No. of community groups	Permanent (n = 315)		Seasonal (n = 308)		χ^2	p-value
	n	%	n	%		
0	120	38.10	173	56.17		
1	54	17.14	91	29.55		
2	63	20.00	31	10.06		
3 or more	78	24.76	13	4.22	76.28	< .0001

SOURCE: Community and Natural Resources Survey 2002.

seasonal homeowners—the state of the lakes. Thus, membership in a lake association may reflect an interest in preserving their property and enjoyment of the lake rather than concern for community-wide issues. Lake associations also offer very little opportunity for seasonal residents to engage with permanent residents since the associations almost entirely consist of vacation homeowners. For many Pine Barrens communities, lake associations can serve as a symbol of the gap between seasonal and permanent residents or between the "haves" and the "have-nots" who can or cannot afford waterfront property. Again, we found that the concentration of seasonal homes around lakeshores creates a social and physical barrier between seasonal and permanent residents. However, it appears that the interests of those seasonal homeowners who belong to more than one community organization extend beyond lake issues. These findings indicate that a community field including seasonal homeowners may be emerging in the Pine Barrens.

Active community participation can also be represented by time spent volunteering for local organizations. The results reported in table 6.6 clearly show that the number of hours spent volunteering for community groups was minor for seasonal homeowners. Nearly 90 percent gave less than an hour of their time per month to community groups. However, as with community organization memberships, there was a subpopulation (10 percent) that was more engaged, volunteering at least one hour per month to community organizations. In one Pine Barrens community, for example, seasonal residents have been an important part of starting a local museum. A permanent resident and local business owner said: "We could not have built the museum here without the leadership, fundraising knowledge, and

TABLE 6.6. Number of hours spent volunteering for community per month

No. of hours	Permanent (n = 322)		Seasonal (n = 303)		χ^2	p-value
	n	%	n	%		
Less than 1	162	50.31	270	89.11		
1 to 4	69	21.43	19	6.27		
5 to 10	51	15.84	12	3.96		
Over 10	40	12.42	2	0.66	113.46	<.0001

SOURCE: Community and Natural Resources Survey 2002.

financial help of our cabin owners and part-time citizens." A small group of committed and engaged seasonal residents has helped to build an important community asset and has spent a significant amount of their time, energy, and assets supporting their new community.

Civic participation is not limited to membership and time spent in community groups. It is also commonly measured by attending public meetings and events, contacting public officials, and working on community projects (see Oliver 2001; Verba, Schlozman, and Brady 1995). Permanent residents were significantly more civically active than seasonal homeowners (see table 6.7). Rates of civic participation by permanent residents were comparable to many national surveys. For example, Ladd (1999) reported that 45 percent of Americans attended a public meeting in the past year (compared to 42 percent of the permanent residents in this study), and 40 percent of Americans worked on a community project during the past year (compared to 44 percent of the permanent residents in this study). But again, the numbers of seasonal homeowners who attended local events (62 percent) and contacted public officials (nearly 45 percent) was noteworthy. Once again

TABLE 6.7. Participation in community events

	Permanent		Seasonal			
	n	%	*n*	%	χ^2	*p*-value
Attended a local event[a]	290	87.61	196	62.22	55.84	<.0001
Contacted a public official[b]	157	47.72	141	44.76	0.57	0.45
Worked on a community project[c]	145	43.94	35	11.15	85.92	<.0001
Attended a public meeting[d]	138	42.07	59	18.73	41.20	<.0001

SOURCE: Community and Natural Resources Survey 2002.

[a] Total *n* for permanent residents = 331 and for seasonal homeowners = 315.
[b] Total *n* for permanent residents = 329 and for seasonal homeowners = 315.
[c] Total *n* for permanent residents = 330 and for seasonal homeowners = 314.
[d] Total *n* for permanent residents = 328 and for seasonal homeowners = 315.

we see a subpopulation of seasonal homeowners who worked on community projects (11 percent of seasonal homeowners) and attended public meetings (nearly 19 percent of seasonal homeowners).

Our key informant interviews reinforced the message that some seasonal homeowners are very engaged in their community. A chamber of commerce leader said that seasonal residents can be members of the chamber and that several are very active in chamber activities during the high season from May to October. The owner of a bookstore said: "Vacation homeowners are active in our book club. We have many locals and summer homeowners both in the club. . . . I also host a book signing once a year featuring our summer resident authors who write about the area. We have many seasonal residents who are artists, writers, photographers who show their work in our stores." Some seasonal homeowners are becoming involved in local events and groups, engaging with their host communities.

The image of the seasonal homeowner as a disengaged and ephemeral tourist does not seem to fairly portray all seasonal homeowners in the Pine Barrens. Instead, there is at least a subpopulation engaged in community affairs: they belonged to community groups, volunteered their time for these groups, and engaged themselves in community activities such as writing public officials and attending public meetings. This subpopulation of seasonal homeowners challenges the image of seasonal homeowners as having shallow and fleeting experiences with their seasonal homes, only using their homes as an escape from reality. Instead, some engage reality in very tangible ways by attending zoning meetings or volunteering for local community projects. These engaged seasonal residents offer further confirmation of findings and theories offered by McIntyre (2006) and other recent works that suggest a more complex understanding of second homeowners is needed.

The next step in our analysis was to examine the effects of different social and demographic factors on community participation. Again, these included length of residence, level of education, income, age, and presence of children in the household, among the other sociodemographic characteristics from our previous analyses. We examined levels of participation in community affairs by seasonal homeowners, using three measures of community participation: membership in community groups, number of hours spent working and volunteering with community groups, and a summated scale of participation in four types of community events or participation (attending a community event like a parade, attending a community meeting, contacting a public official, and working on a community project).

Once again our analysis showed that the number of days seasonal residents spend at their second home significantly impacts their community participation. Seasonal residents who spend more time at their homes are involved in more community groups, volunteering in the community, and attending community events.[3] Spending more time at their homes allows these seasonal residents to become active, contributing members of their communities. We also again see the dividing effects of waterfront property, as seasonal residents with waterfront homes are much less likely to attend community events. Repeatedly we find that there is a social barrier between residents who have waterfront property and those who do not.

SUMMARY

The analysis of local social ties and community participation of permanent and seasonal residents reinforces our findings regarding community attachment: seasonal residents have distinct relationships with their host communities, but these relationships are more complex and deeper than commonly assumed. Seasonal residents did tend to have more limited social circles and generally less participation in community affairs, but in specific areas, contacting a public official and cross-group interactions, they were actually more engaged with their communities than permanent residents.

Even without the potential difficulties of seasonal residency, rural life can already create obstacles to healthy community development by limiting the social interaction of residents because of low population density, the necessity of meeting needs nonlocally, and high levels of inequality. Wilkinson (1991, 59) wrote:

> Community, as argued earlier, requires a locality where people can meet their daily needs together and a local society where social contacts can produce a holistic structure. . . . Rural life works against the community field by restricting the probability that a complete local society will develop and persist in the

---

3. The full model for volunteering at least one hour per month to community organizations did not approach significance, though the number of days spent was significant in the model (see appendix B). The nonsignificance of the model indicates that the selected variables cumulatively do a very poor job of explaining variation in volunteering patterns. This is perhaps not surprising given the social, psychological, and microsociological literature that has explored complex reasoning behind volunteering contributions (Putnam 2000).

immediate area of residence . . . in two ways. First distance restricts the kinds
of contacts needed to build community bonds among residents of the local
society as a whole. Second, poverty and inequality . . . can produce cleavages
that block and distort community interaction.

Wilkinson's theory would support the conclusion that any feature of rural
life that aggravates the barriers to community already present would only
further discourage community engagement. In many ways, seasonal housing development could magnify the interactional obstacles already present
in rural areas. Second-home owners have only seasonal interaction with
community members, maintain close ties with resources outside of the community, and have generally higher incomes and education than their permanent neighbors. The employment opportunities generated by seasonal
housing development are generally low paying, lacking stability or diversity
(Coppock 1977a; Green et al. 1996; Jensen and Field 2004; Visser 2004).
It is also possible, however, that seasonal residents serve to reduce these
obstacles by at least temporarily increasing density and by their personal
and associational ties in the community.

In rural communities, scholars and planners often assume that demographic differences between seasonal and permanent residents, particularly
income, are responsible for social tensions in communities and lack of engagement. The results of this study do not support this inference. Demographic
characteristics failed to explain how residents engage their community, suggesting complex social and psychological elements influencing seasonal residents. Instead, the number of days that seasonal residents spend at their
home continues to have the largest effect on how they engage with their
new communities. Seasonal residents who spend more days at the home
have higher levels of attachment, social ties, and community engagement and
begin to resemble permanent residents more than other seasonal residents.
This replicates findings by Stedman (2006) and others who find substantial
diversity among the seasonal resident population and some frequent seasonal visitors who have relationships marked similarity to their permanent
neighbors. There are, however, clearly demonstrated differences between
the permanent and seasonal resident populations, in both levels of community engagement and significant factors affecting this engagement. Seasonal
residents have very different relationships with their communities than their
permanent neighbors, and this can have real implications for planners and
residents.

CONCLUSION

In this chapter we delved further into social organization, examining both social networks and community participation. The growth of new and distinct populations of seasonal residents in the consumption landscape of the Pine Barrens has significantly affected these forms of social organization. The new population of seasonal residents has led to a downgrading of some social interaction and community engagement, but we also demonstrated some positive transformations of social organization by a subgroup of very involved seasonal residents. Individual features of residents, particularly the number of days spent at their second home, shape the relationship between population changes and social organization changes.

chapter 7

Resource Management and Land-Use Planning

Changing Communities

This is an interesting survey. Having recently completed a related survey for [another project] I am glad to see you asking the right questions about development. You are obviously digging deeper than "surveyists" usually go. Bravo.

—Community and Natural Resources Survey respondent

As Pine Barrens rural communities have undergone rapid changes in population and social organization, these transformations have had impacts on the management of natural resources and the environment. Population growth and residential development profoundly alter the physical attributes of the landscape. Adjacent public lands and natural areas are particularly susceptible to unchecked growth and resultant landscape disturbance. Residential development on the borders of public lands alters the composition and configuration of ecological communities, creating a landscape mosaic that impedes the flows of plant and animal populations across the landscape. In addition, such discontinuities in the landscape can make it much more difficult to coordinate and achieve ecosystem management practices such as ecosystem restoration, reintroduction of endangered species, and fire management. Land-use planners, public land managers, and the residents of the rapidly growing Pine Barrens are beginning to realize the effects of this disruption of management and natural processes on their regional environmental quality, recreational space, and quality of life.

While rural Pine Barrens communities have undergone dramatic transformations and restructuring, so too have the policies and practices of natural resources management. Natural resources management is increasingly informed by the idea of ecosystem management, a core element of which is the management of large land areas defined by ecological boundaries rather than legal or political boundaries. This necessitates collaboration and collective decision making among a broad array of social and political stakeholders (Christensen et al. 1996; Cortner and Moote 1999; Grumbine 1994; Yaffee 1999). In addition, active engagement of multiple constituencies in collaborative management efforts has been found to be critically important in tempering conflicts and resulting political gridlock that characterize many resource management debates (Brick, Snow, and Van de Wetering 2001; Cortner and Moote 1999; Daniels and Walker 1995; Kemmis 1990; Wondoleck and Yaffee 2000).

The potential for conflict between seasonal and permanent residents is present monthly in the county zoning board meetings of the study area. A meeting held in the spring of 2006 well illustrates the complex tensions and divisions in these rapidly transforming communities. The zoning committee convened a public meeting to hear a variety of proposals for growth and development characterizing many of the changes typical in natural amenity-based communities. Debate surrounding the approval of a planned multistage senior living community on a lakefront highlighted the tensions between seasonal and permanent homeowners. The family whose land was being sold for development sat quietly next to the developers as one outspoken neighbor voiced her discontent with the plan:

> [The landowners] don't care about this development because they're not going to have to live with it! After they move away, we're going to be the ones who have to look at this ugly nursing home every day! And another thing, why do these meetings always have to take place in the middle of the week? Most of my neighbors are seasonal folks who can't be here during the week. Shouldn't they get to have a say in what gets built on *their* lake? (Retired Washburn County resident)

These tensions over the future development and growth of the Pine Barrens are very real struggles over self-definition and ideology for local residents.

Improving our understanding of the attitudes that seasonal homeowners hold toward the management of public lands and shoreline management regulations is important for several reasons. First, because many seasonal homeowners intend to relocate or retire to their seasonal home, their attitudes provide insight into possible changes and challenges to predominant community views and priorities for resource management (American Society

1976; Beyers and Nelson 2000; Girard and Gartner 1993; Marans and Wellman 1978). Second, seasonal homeowners are a potentially important group of stakeholders in resource management decision making. Seasonal homeowners in many areas tend to be better educated and more wealthy than permanent residents, and they may have the skills, experience, and resources to influence decision making, particularly by contacting public officials individually or through local citizens groups such as lake organizations (American Society 1976; Klessig 1973). During an interview, a Pine Barrens county employee illustrated the important influence of seasonal residents when he said: "We welcome summer residents into many of our committees. They are very active members and local leaders." He spoke of their experience in business and politics that gives them the skills to influence county decisions and committees. Third, natural resource management increasingly emphasizes the importance of community involvement and collaboration, especially in areas where resource and land-use control is shared among numerous institutional and community actors (Cortner and Moote 1999; Endter-Wada et al. 1998; Healey 1997; Lane 2002; Wondoleck and Yaffee 2000). Thus, as resource managers adopt a more collaborative and community-based management approach, seasonal homeowners may become increasingly important stakeholders.

History of Conflicts in the Northwoods

Development of seasonal homes in northern Wisconsin has previously spurred conflict concerning local development and land-use issues. Most people who purchase land in northwestern Wisconsin do so for reasons related to recreation and outdoor amenities while few purchased land for farming or timber production (Green et al. 1996; Kummerow, Moyer, and Jordahl 1981; Marcouiller et al. 1996). These different conceptions of local natural resources can lead to conflict over future management. Conflicts and differences between seasonal and permanent residents have also been found in other amenity-rich regions of northern Wisconsin. For example, research in Forest County found that seasonal homeowners were primarily concerned about environmental issues and were more supportive of land-use planning while questioning the benefits of economic development. In contrast, local residents were more concerned with increasing the tax base and economic development (Green et al. 1996).

In addition, sometimes tourism development has created feelings of control imposed by outsiders. Some suggest that there is a sense among residents that they have to produce an image that tourists want of northern Wisconsin. According to Bob Kurth, University of Wisconsin–Extension, visitors "have a certain mental image of what the North is all about" (Gough 1997, 226). Seasonal homes surround most lakes, and according to interviews with long-term residents, some find it harder to afford the cost of living in their own communities. One permanent resident told us: "I could no longer afford to live on the lake so I moved into town. To live here all year we must have at least two jobs." Many local businesses reduce their hours October through April, and some even close for the entire slow season. Local residents are becoming economically dependent on tourists, which can lead to frustrated responses and conflict (Gough 1997).

Wisconsin's cities, villages, counties, and towns have the authority to make various land-use decisions that ultimately determine how future growth is configured on the landscape—including zoning, development review, and utility extension. Further, with Wisconsin's Comprehensive Planning Legislation passed in 1999, communities throughout the state are required to make land-use decisions (zoning, plat approval) consistent with a comprehensive plan. This legislation, popularly referred to as "Smart Growth," requires that a community make decisions consistent with an adopted plan containing each of nine required elements (including agricultural, natural and cultural resources; economic development; housing; transportation; and economic development) by the end of 2010.

The Smart Growth planning process requires and encourages broad public participation. The state administers a program that provides grants for communities to undertake this planning process. As a result, many communities throughout Wisconsin, including rural towns that might not normally have engaged in such a formal planning process, are undertaking comprehensive planning processes. Several communities in the Pine Barrens study area—including towns and both counties—are writing comprehensive plans to guide their future growth and development. Several communities have also joined in some capacity with the Northwest Regional Planning Commission (NWRPC), the oldest planning commission in Wisconsin. "Working cooperatively with Counties, Local Units of Government, Tribal Nations and other regional organizations comprising the District, Northwest Regional Planning Commission will assist in improving and enhancing the economic conditions in the area to provide a positive economic impact and improve the region's economic prosperity" (Northwest 2008). This process necessarily engages the public in a discourse about the future growth and development of communities. With public involvement comes the need to balance a range of interests, values, and goals that are as different as the individuals in a community. In communities with perceived or real factions of newcomers and long-term residents, seasonal and year-round residents, this balancing of interests can be challenging for the planners facilitating the process and the local government decision makers who ultimately implement (or choose not to implement) strategies to manage growth and development.

Previous research provides evidence that some community divisions and conflicts already exist in the Pine Barrens. Stonebraker (2003) found that the comprehensive planning process in the town of Scott, located in Burnett County, created substantial conflict. Conflict among residents was largely attributed to different values about land and property, with new residents more supportive of planning, regulations, and preservation (Stonebraker 2003). In addition, some public officials feel there is an increasingly vocal absentee landowner population protesting tax assessments and local projects (Luedeke 1995). Marcouiller et al. (1996) propose that long-term residents in the Pine Barrens, having strong social and economic ties to the region, are more supportive of managing the area as a "working landscape" that is actively managed for agriculture and forestry than newer or seasonal residents.

As the Pine Barrens undergoes these crucial changes and struggles to address the new demands of resource management and planning, it is increasingly important to have a good understanding of where the different rural constituencies stand on the issues. In this chapter, we analyze the opinions of seasonal and permanent residents, long-term and recent migrants, and other potentially important divides in the Pine Barrens communities. Unlike many of these previous studies, however, our findings offer some unexpected optimism about shared priorities among residents. In order to address the ecological and planning concerns at hand, the analysis in this chapter differs slightly from analysis used in the previous chapters, reflecting a distinct ecological focus and a concurrently distinct literature of interest.

Divided Opinions?

Our analysis suggests that there are some differences between responses to land-use controls, planning, and growth management between seasonal and permanent residents and long-term and newcomer residents, but not to the extent that planners and land managers might postulate. In addition, while differences do exist between seasonal and permanent residents, overall support for land-use planning tools among all citizens is quite high. In the following sections we examine attitudes toward public land management, perceptions of community change, perceived need for growth management, private property rights attitudes, and the preferred scale of planning and management. We conclude by discussing the implications of our findings for the planning process in these Pine Barrens communities.

Public Land Management Priorities

First, we examined seasonal homeowners and permanent residents' attitudes toward public land management (see table 7.1). We asked residents to rank different management goals (e.g., hunting opportunities, timber production) in level of importance. Seasonal and permanent residents have a substantial gap in their attitudes toward the use of public lands for timber production and hunting. Permanent residents placed more importance on managing public lands for timber and hunting opportunities, while many seasonal residents saw these goals as unimportant for local public lands. However, there were no statistically significant differences between permanent residents and seasonal homeowners in their attitudes toward recreational opportunities, endangered species protection, wilderness values, beauty and aesthetics, land-use planning, or shoreline regulations. For both types

TABLE 7.1. Importance of public land management goals by type of resident

	Percentage of respondents rating management goal as very or somewhat important		Percentage of respondents rating management goal as very or somewhat unimportant	
	Permanent	Seasonal	Permanent	Seasonal
Timber production	80.63	74.84	6.56	16.55
Hunting opportunities	79.19	68.93	8.39	14.24
Recreational opportunities	82.87	88.31	4.68	3.25
Wilderness values	91.25	94.79	2.19	0.33
Endangered species protection	83.80	83.55	6.55	5.17
Beauty and aesthetics	92.55	96.45	0.31	0.00

SOURCE: Community and Natural Resources Survey 2002.

of residents, the management goals with the highest mean levels of importance were the noncommodity, "natural amenity" management goals: beauty
and aesthetics, wilderness values, endangered species protection, and recreational opportunities.

Further examination of attitudes toward public land management goals
revealed that residents, regardless of seasonal versus permanent residence,
placed more importance on amenity, noncommodity management goals
than on commodity goals. It also appears that respondents supported all of
the management goals for the public lands. In other words, residents would
like to see the public lands managed to provide a wide range of goods and
benefits and did not seem to see managing at least some public lands for
timber production as incompatible with managing public lands for wilderness values. It is interesting to note that among seasonal residents there
was still relatively strong support for managing public lands for traditional
extractive goals of timber and hunting. While seasonal residents were more
supportive of amenity-related management goals such as aesthetics and wilderness, they were not widely opposed to managing for timber and hunting.

Development, Northwoods Character, and Community Change

Next we examine the attitudes of seasonal and permanent residents toward
different aspects of community change (see table 7.2). Most of the residents,
both permanent and seasonal (67 percent), feel that development is causing
a loss of the "Northwoods character." At the same time, fewer than 17 percent of all community members would agree that the more their community changes, the happier they are with it as a place to live. Considered
together, these results indicate an overall negative perception of community
change spurred by development. However, residents do not overwhelmingly
cite recreational home development as a factor diminishing their satisfac-
tion with their community. Nearly 45 percent of community members feel
that recreational home development is having a good effect on their community. Further, most are relatively neutral regarding the effect of new people
on their community. The above suggests an apparent disconnect between
acknowledgment of "erosion of place" (as indicated by concern over loss
of Northwoods character and concern about community change) and the
attribution of this to housing and population growth, notably a failure to
connect this growth and change to proliferating seasonal and recreational
homes. Or alternatively, the belief that the positive economic implications
of new and recreational home development supersede the adverse effects.

TABLE 7.2. Views on growth and development

	Percentage who agree	Percentage who disagree
Development is causing a loss of the Northwoods character	68.6	16.4
The more this community changes, the happier I am with it as a place to live	16.5	52.8
Recreational home development is having a good effect on this community	44.0	30.3
New people moving to the area over the past few years are having a bad effect on this area	28.8	31.1
Public policies to manage growth and development are needed to help slow down the pace of change in northwestern Wisconsin	55.8	23.4

SOURCE: Community and Natural Resources Survey 2002.

But what about differences between the groups of residents? Do seasonal and permanent residents have different attitudes toward development? What about long-term residents versus newcomers? In contrast to many other studies that find seasonal residents oppose development and change, we find that more year-round residents agree that development is causing a loss of the Northwoods character (see table 7.3). Similarly, more long-term residents agree that development is causing a loss of Northwoods character. In addition, the long-term residents feel more adversely affected by change, as indicated by their higher probability of disagreeing that the "more their community changes the happier I am with it as a place to live." To this end, it appears that the "erosion of place" and concerns over a loss of identity are more salient to year-round than seasonal residents and to long-term residents than to newcomers. This runs contrary to Cockerham and Blevins's (1977) study of Jackson Hole, Wyoming, wherein newcomers more frequently expressed concern over growth. In our study, long-term and year-round residents tend to express more negative reactions to growth and community change. The notion that long-term and year-round residents are more invested in a locale both in terms of time, historical connection to community, and share of personal wealth in property may explain this negative perception of community change.

TABLE 7.3. Views on growth and development by type of resident

| | Percentage who agree | | | | Percentage who disagree | | | |
| | Year-round | | Seasonal | | Year-round | | Seasonal | |
	Long-term	Newcomer	Long-term	Newcomer	Long-term	Newcomer	Long-term	Newcomer
Development is causing a loss of the Northwoods character	72.7	78.0	67.04	55.7	12.7	15.3	17.9	22.1
The more this community changes, the happier I am with it as a place to live	16.1	27.4	10.2	16.2	56.6	46.2	59.3	44.6
Recreational home development is having a good effect on this community	44.6	44.4	34.8	56.1	34.8	31.3	33.7	18.9
New people moving to the area over the past few years are having a bad effect on this area	36.3	23.1	30.3	20.5	30.9	40.2	24.7	31.8
Public policies to manage growth and development are needed to help slow down the pace of change in northwestern Wisconsin	57.8	55.9	57.1	52.7	22.3	29.7	20.9	22.1

SOURCE: Community and Natural Resources Survey 2002.

Growth Management, Rural Landscapes, and Public Policy

Negative perceptions of change, new residents, and recreational homes do not translate into a perceived need for growth management among long-term or year-round residents (see table 7.4). While overall more than 55 percent of all community members agree that public policies are needed to slow the growth and development, there is no difference between seasonal and permanent residents or between long-term and newcomer residents. Whereas long-term and year-round residents seem to recognize the adverse effects of growth and development, they may not agree with public policies as the appropriate way to deal with it. Indeed, our results show that year-round and long-term residents have less confidence in the efficacy of public policies to mitigate the impacts of growth and development than seasonal residents or newcomers. Overall, more than 55 percent of community members agreed that managing growth and development would help slow down the pace of change in their community, while fewer than 17 percent disagreed with this statement. However, seasonal residents are more likely than year-round residents to agree that growth management efforts would be effective in slowing down the pace of change in their community.

Further, the majority of residents (75 percent) agreed that public policies managing growth and development help maintain a clean environment. Few community members disagreed with that statement. But again, seasonal residents are more likely to agree with the utility of public policies in safeguarding environmental values. These results suggest that whereas long-term and year-round residents perceive the adverse effects of growth and development to a greater extent than their new or seasonal counterparts, they have less confidence in public policies to effectively manage growth and development.

These results are similar to previous studies wherein new residents were more likely than traditional residents to support public policies that institute environmental controls or land-use planning measures (Blahna 1990; Graber 1974; Marcouiller et al. 1996). Taking this a step further, our analyses suggest that residency type (seasonal versus year-round) is a more important predictor than length of residency. Like M. Smith and Krannich (1998, 2000), who demonstrated that both long-term residents and newcomers report high importance of preserving existing community ways of life, we demonstrate that residents do recognize the problems of unrestrained growth and development. However, type of residence can be more important for predicting broad support for growth management policies. Although

TABLE 7.4. Anticipated consequences of growth management

	Percentage who agree				Percentage who disagree			
	Year-round		Seasonal		Year-round		Seasonal	
	Long-term	Newcomer	Long-term	Newcomer	Long-term	Newcomer	Long-term	Newcomer
Managing growth and development would help slow the pace of change in this community	47.6	56.4	63.1	61.1	21.4	18.0	14.2	12.2
Public policies to manage growth and development help maintain a clean environment, including air and water	71.9	78.0	79.1	74.0	14.1	7.6	8.5	11.5

SOURCE: Community and Natural Resources Survey 2002.

year-round residents perceive change and growth as a threat to a greater extent, similar to previous studies in Wisconsin (Marcouiller et al. 1996), we show that seasonal residents are more likely to support growth management public policies.

Private Property Rights Values and the Environment

A strong private property rights ethic can run counter to support for public policies to reign in growth and may explain why there is resistance to public policies for management and change. Often the support of growth management is tempered by a strong private property rights ethic. Growth management, land-use controls, and planning are seen as impinging on individual rights. Interestingly, over 68 percent of all community members agreed that it is acceptable to restrict private property rights in order to protect the environment (see table 7.5); fewer than 25 percent disagreed. In contrast, our second question concerning private property rights was much more polarized: more than half of residents disagreed with the statement "use of private land should be based on what the owner wants, rather than restricted by regulations," while nearly half agreed. Very few were neutral toward this statement. This inconsistency is difficult to understand, but may be attributed to the specificity of the first statement: perhaps a limitation of private property rights for a given purpose (in order to protect the environment) conjures less negative connotations to the respondent than a restrictions where the purpose is vague and the regulations run contrary to the owner "wants."

As predicted, year-round residents hold a stronger private property rights ethic than seasonal residents, but this is only the case for one of the two questions. Again, this provides some support for the disconnect between negative perceptions of community change and lack of support for public policies to address it; such policies are often seen as counter to private property rights, an ethic that year-round residents tend to hold strongly. Contrary to our expectation, long-term residents and newcomers do not differ in terms of their private property rights ethic. Following from Cockerham and Blevins's (1977) study of Jackson Hole, Wyoming, we expected that land-use controls would seem more threatening to long-term and year-round residents than to new and seasonal residents because of the percentage of their total net worth invested in their Pine Barrens property, and that a more profound private property rights ethic would be hinged to their rural origin. Instead, there were no significant differences in the private property rights values of long-term and newcomer residents.

TABLE 7.5. Private property rights ethic

	Percentage who agree				Percentage who disagree			
	Year-round		Seasonal		Year-round		Seasonal	
	Long-term	Newcomer	Long-term	Newcomer	Long-term	Newcomer	Long-term	Newcomer
It is acceptable to restrict private property rights in order to protect the environment	68.3	72.0	67.0	67.2	23.4	22.0	27.4	21.4
Use of private land should be based on what the owner wants, rather than restricted by regulations	48.0	41.9	33.2	33.3	42.7	51.3	60.0	59.7

SOURCE: Community and Natural Resources Survey 2002.

In summary, the overall response to community change, attitudes toward managing growth and development, anticipated consequences of managing growth and development, and a private property rights ethic seem to provide a consistent message. Respondents overall perceive change induced by growth and development as a threat to the character of their community as well as their quality of life. The majority of community members support policies to manage growth and development. However, this level of support may be compromised by a strong private property rights ethic. Based on previous studies and our findings, we might expect permanent and long-term residents to support public policies to control growth and development since they are the most sensitive to its negative consequences. However, because they lack confidence in the efficacy of growth management policies and have a stronger private property rights ethic, permanent and long-term residents do not support public policies to manage growth and development. Optimistically, community members overall did not blame new residents and recreational homes for the negative consequences of growth and development.

Scale of Planning

The regional context of the Pine Barrens in the Northwoods also has implications for the mode of planning employed. The Pine Barrens region, valued for its stock of natural amenities, is ecologically defined, but politically fragmented. The ecological region of the Pine Barrens spans many townships, counties, unincorporated areas, and other political entities. The scale at which planning takes place—on the townships/community, county, or regional level—is therefore an important issue in the region. Community based planning, by virtue of its community rather than regional scale, would provide less comprehensive and consistent solutions for the ecological and economic resources of this unique region. In terms of scale of planning for future growth and development and promoting a regional approach, there is an overwhelming amount of support for cooperation of communities, with nearly 75 percent of all community members agreeing that there needs to be more cooperation among communities in planning for future growth and development (see table 7.6). This is meaningful in terms of Wisconsin's Comprehensive Planning Legislation (1999), which requires intergovernmental cooperation as an element of an individual communities planning effort. Further, it bodes well for the regional scope of planning that is required where economic, ecological, and social variables cross-jurisdictional

TABLE 7.6. Attitudes toward community cooperation

	Percentage who agree						Percentage who disagree					
	Year-round		Seasonal		Year-round		Seasonal					
	Long-term	Newcomer	Long-term	Newcomer	Long-term	Newcomer	Long-term	Newcomer				
There needs to be more cooperation among communities in planning for growth and development in Northwestern Wisconsin	76.2	73.5	76.3	64.1	6.8	4.3	2.3	6.9				

SOURCE: Community and Natural Resources Survey 2002.

boundaries, as is the case in the Pine Barrens region. We see this cooperation happening already in a portion of the study area—Washburn County. Here, county and cooperative town-level planning is underway concurrently (NWRCP 2000).

Interestingly, most residents prefer county-level control of future growth and development. This is another positive indicator for regional-scale planning in the Pine Barrens. This level of support may be indicative of the joint county-local planning efforts already underway in Washburn County, as well as the strong county and Northwest Regional Planning Commission presence in Burnett County. However, the preferred level of governance among seasonal and year-round residents was different. Year-round residents were more likely than seasonal residents to prefer local or individual control of governance of future growth and development. This is not surprising, as year-round residents may have less experience with regional and metropolitan government because they live in a predominantly rural area and because they likely have local economic interests. On the other hand, the great majority of seasonal residents originate from urban areas, in particular the Twin Cities metropolitan area. In the Minneapolis/St. Paul area, there is a strong presence of regional metropolitan governance and cooperation. By virtue of this experience, it makes sense that the seasonal residents would be supportive of higher levels of control.

Implications for the Comprehensive Planning Process and Growth Management

Overall, our results provide support for the planning that is currently underway in the Pine Barrens, as well as expansions of current efforts under the Comprehensive Planning Legislation. Whereas overall levels of support for planning are moderate to high among community members, it is necessary to consider the differences of support among residents, particularly the lack of faith in public policies shared by some permanent residents, to understand how growth management might play out in the region.

In addition to recognizing the differences between groups, the very definition of citizenship can provoke tension and conflict surrounding planning in rural areas. The constructs of formal and substantive citizenship hold particular relevance for rural areas experiencing rapid rates of seasonal and recreational home development. Seasonal residents typically are legal residents of another jurisdiction; thus policy makers must consider the extent to which these residents should have a voice in local decision making.

Whereas seasonal residents do not have a voice in the form of a vote, they certainly have an interest and ability to affect and be affected by local politics, local government decisions, planning, and other local affairs. Seasonal residents, though not formal citizens, may be active in local organizations, in particular lake associations and other environmental groups. The involvement of seasonal residents in these community groups and stakes in local development issues may lend credence to their "substantive citizenship" and call into question the broad, social meaning of citizenship (Sandercock 1998). Our findings demonstrate that seasonal residents do hold somewhat different views on growth management. Whereas they may be less likely to perceive the adverse impacts of growth and development, they have more confidence in the growth management process and therefore could be an asset to the planning process. Even where traditional and new residents may express some similar concerns about growth and change in their communities, planners must seek to understand whether these truly are shared underlying concerns, or just a shared rhetoric toward preserving rural character (Dubbink 1984).

When comparing seasonal and permanent residents, the communities of the Pine Barrens seem less contested than one might expect. There was a fairly high level of convergence between seasonal and permanent residents in their attitudes toward growth management, land use, and the management of public lands. There was also more support for growth management and land-use controls among permanent residents than the literature suggested. Support, however, was not overwhelming as sizable minorities oppose growth management and property restrictions. Residents of the Pine Barrens place more importance on the natural amenity values of the landscape around them and were supportive of growth management in order to help preserve those natural amenities.

The "culture clash" between urban seasonal homeowners and rural permanent residents did not appear to be as dramatic as one might expect, at least in terms of attitudes toward natural resources management. The influx of seasonal homeowners as part-time residents, and for some later in retirement as permanent residents, may not be as disruptive as the existing literature suggests. This could be due to the long history of cottages and resorts in the Northwoods, dating back to the beginning of the twentieth century (Murphy 1931), to the steady conversion of seasonal homes to permanent residences, and to the unique features of seasonal homeowners in the Pine Barrens such as previous residency and, relative to second homeowners in the West, more moderate incomes. Nearly 18 percent of current permanent residents in our study were once seasonal homeowners, and 47 percent of current seasonal homeowners indicate that they were likely to establish permanent residence in the Pine Barrens sometime in the future. The existence of common attitudes toward some aspects of public land management holds promise that community changes and shifts created by seasonal homeowners may not be as disruptive as many fear. This has important implications for community members, local officials, resource managers, and planners, as broad public support for growth management and resource management goals currently exists, contrary to popular perception. Perhaps the more important issue facing communities in the Pine Barrens is finding agreement on the role of seasonal homeowners in local governance than on the substantive issues of resource management and land-use planning.

The research on attitudes toward resource management on public lands in the twenty-first century is predicated on understanding the changing face of American communities. Rural regions in which there are considerable amounts of public lands are becoming magnets for urban developments and gateway communities. In short, the urban/wildland interface stretches particularly far from urban centers where natural amenities and seasonal homes abound. As natural resources management policy becomes increasingly collaborative in nature, it should be encouraging to resource managers that there is at least some common ground among the diverse residents and seasonal homeowners in such places as the Pine Barrens. However, research on rural change and rural restructuring is only just beginning to recognize the impacts that seasonal homeowners can have on communities and natural resources, and that systematic and longitudinal research on seasonal homeowners is needed.

Conclusion

Previously, we described the changing composition of Pine Barrens residents and the new consumption landscape of rural natural amenity-based communities. The same new residents who are reshaping the economic and social fabric of the Pine Barrens communities are also reshaping the debates about the natural environment. There is a clear recognition by permanent and seasonal residents alike that the physical landscape of the Pine Barrens is being dramatically altered alongside the cultural landscape. Development on the boundaries of public lands is likewise altering the migration patterns of wildlife such as elk and wolves and creating fragmented habitat. There is a convergence among the new and long-term residents and seasonal residents in the belief that wildlife are indeed an amenity asset of the Pine Barrens and that regional planning can promote protection of landscapes and these amenity assets. Residents' values suggest that non-extractive resource management, such as protection of habitat for wildlife and endangered species, may gradually gain a foothold on local, state, and federal decision making on natural resource management policies.

chapter 8

Patterns on the Land

T HE SOCIOLOGY OF NATURAL RESOURCES involves the study of
the interaction of human societies with their environment, specifically the variety of patterns of definition, discovery, and use of
natural resources. Rural communities, in particular, have historically been
closely tied to their natural resources through dependence on extractive industries such as mining, fishing, forestry, and agriculture. Throughout this
book, we have told the story of how many rural communities have shifted
this dependence on natural resources. Rural communities rich in natural
amenities are still dependent on their natural resource base, but now many
have transformed into consumption landscapes in which natural resources
are valued for their recreation and aesthetic values. We have told the story
of the Pine Barrens of northern Wisconsin as they have made their own
transformation: the new urban migrants, seasonal residents, and retirees who
have moved into former forestry communities, and the values they have
brought with them.

The story of northwestern Wisconsin and its transformation from a production landscape to a consumption landscape is unique, but it also reflects
a common pattern in many rural American communities. Rural areas rich
in popular natural amenities such as lakes, rivers, mountains, forests, and
natural scenery are growing in population from the in-migration of urban
residents, retirees, and seasonal residents. These communities are no longer
"company towns" whose employment and economic base was dominated
by mining, forestry, or agriculture; instead, tourism, real estate, and hospi-
tality services are increasingly important aspects of their economic growth.
In both eras, these communities are intimately dependent on their natural

resources, although contemporary communities are largely dependent on their non-extractive aesthetic and recreational values. These cultural landscapes have transformed production landscapes in which natural resources are defined in terms of their extractive values to consumption landscapes where natural resources are valued for their aesthetic and recreational potential and the environmental services of the land are emphasized. What is consumed in non-extractive rural communities is landscape itself rather than its extractive outputs.

Northwestern Wisconsin is now home to more diverse rural residents, including seasonal residents and retirees who have migrated to take advantage of the amenities offered by the region's natural resources. Instead of conflict and tension among different groups of residents, however, most residents have high levels of community attachment and many important local friendship and family ties, and there is a subgroup of seasonal residents who seem to be very dedicated to their new communities. Likewise, many important attitudes about the management of natural resources and a vision for the future of the Northwoods are shared among diverse community members. The transformation from a production to consumption landscape has not undermined the well-being of these communities in northwestern Wisconsin, providing reason for optimism for other rural communities experiencing similar conversions.

BROADER IMPLICATIONS

As we end our story of the people and places in Wisconsin's Pine Barrens, it is appropriate that we return to exploring patterns on the land more broadly. The landscapes of the Pine Barrens, like rural landscapes throughout the United States and globally, have been transformed by the changing relationship of communities to their natural resources. Loggers and farmers once saw the Pine Barrens as an extractive paradise, only to have their dreams swept aside by indiscriminate logging practices, nutrient deficient soils, inhospitable climates, and short growing seasons. Yet the Pine Barrens—with its abundance of lakes, second-growth forests, wetlands, and wildlife—has regained its prominence as a natural resource treasure. Both the production landscape of extraction and the consumption landscape based on natural amenity attractions are dependent upon the natural resource base of the Pine Barrens. Like others (see Mather 2001 and Walker and Fortmann 2003 for more discussion), we have used the terms *production* and *consumption landscapes* to differentiate the dominant livelihoods and community structures of rural people and rural places over time. The Pine Barrens remains an important cultural landscape, although quite different from that constructed by its nineteenth- and early twentieth-century residents. Rural cultural landscapes—defined as production or consumption landscapes or some combination of both—help us understand the nature of changes taking place in rural northern Wisconsin.

These lessons are, however, not limited to Wisconsin's Pine Barrens. Natural amenity-rich communities are being transformed across the United States and around the world. Small towns like Wimberley in the central Texas Hill Country are now home to luxury bed and breakfasts, vineyards owned by retired California attorneys, and million-dollar "cabins" on the banks of the Guadalupe River. Nearby Kerrville, Texas, is one of the fastest-growing retirement destinations in the nation, offering the rolling hills and scenic rivers of the Hill Country alongside cutting-edge medical facilities. The emergence of a consumption landscape is not limited to the ski resorts of Colorado or the mansions of the Hamptons on Long Island. Many nonmetropolitan communities from Maine to Oregon continue to experience population growth, primarily through in-migration of residents from urban areas, greater than those of the nation at large. Other communities with similar landscapes, natural resource amenities, and histories are also experiencing these changes.

This study adds an understanding of the role of temporary residents (living on lakes, in the forests, or adjacent to public lands) to existing discussions of rural people, places, and landscapes. We described how the landscapes these residents helped create reflect their cultural imprint on forest and lake communities. Such communities are no longer dominated by extractive industries associated with production landscapes. We have come a long way since our first chapters chronicling rural change, yet the principles remain: rural people and communities are intertwined with the natural resources and landscapes they create. Our work extends the basic script of rural people and places to include seasonal residents and has merit for others studying twenty-first-century rural landscapes. However, if our analysis of the Pine Barrens ended there, we would not have fully completed our tasks. Rather, we close by focusing on three broad themes scientists and policy makers should consider as the twenty-first century continues to unfold: (1) embracing integrated and collaborative schemes for managing natural resources and public lands where second-home development is occurring, (2) building on the common values of seasonal and permanent residents for managing rural development, and (3) recognizing that diversity within rural communities can create human capital that supports community well-being.

COLLABORATIVE MANAGEMENT: BROADENING THE BASE

Communities like those in the Wisconsin Northwoods, which has over half a million acres of public forest (Hammer et al. 2009), are increasingly intertwined with neighboring public lands. For too long park and forest managers have stood sentry to protect the resources within a park or forest, marking the boundary between the park and surrounding communities and neglecting the people and communities that border their domains. They have implicitly ignored the happenings outside of their direct purview of responsibility, but twenty-first-century environmental change does not allow the dismissal of land-use actions next door. Public land mangers at all levels of government must engage their neighbors to find solutions for community development on the boundaries of public lands and habitat management. In an essay of the future of parks, Destry Jarvis (2000) suggests that "park managers break out from hiding behind statutory invisible walls and become ambassadors of rural development. In doing so, the National Park Service becomes proactive stakeholders influencing the direction of rural development on neighboring lands and a practitioner applying Leopold's land ethic" (221).

Collaborative resource management is one approach involving the cooperation and collaboration of land managers with community members from neighboring areas. Within the collaborative management model, public managers are encouraged to work with the variety of neighbors and users who are stakeholders in the management of public lands. The central premise of collaborative management is that for successful public land management, managers need to understand the importance of incorporating local community opinions, concerns, and knowledge into their natural resource management plans. Although the collaborative model is not new, U.S. public land managers have been reluctant to embrace it. The twenty-first century is marked by the emergence of even more new stakeholder bases in the communities surrounding public lands, however, and developing dialogue between these groups is now essential to implementing natural resource plans. Precisely because public land management agencies are now more closely connected to their adjacent neighbors, genuine collaborative efforts are needed to determine the best ways to balance the needs of neighboring communities with those of the broader national interest. Parks are no longer islands with vast open space separating development from land protection but rather a magnet for natural amenity development like that of the Pine Barrens.

Because of the growing popularity of collaborative management plans, neighboring communities now play a larger role in developing many public land management plans. However, conflicting interests and concerns with public lands are often evident in communities neighboring public lands. Communities once dependent upon public lands for employment and income associated with timber production may now be home to residents who value the land for its amenities and recreational opportunities. This shift from production to consumption landscapes has generated new and often conflicting conceptions of the relationship between public lands and the community. Some of these changes have been examined in the "New West" literature that focused on the changing employment base, rapid population growth, and altered sociodemographic profiles of such places. Often these studies reflected the migration of individuals with high levels of income and education into natural amenity areas (Rengert and Lang 2001; Shumway and Otterstrum 2001; Taylor 2004). These changes in rural communities make developing management goals for public land challenging.

Public land managers need to do more than simply acknowledge the presence of this new group of seasonal residents when creating management goals and plans. They need to involve them in the development of the plans. Since the public is playing a greater role in management decisions, and seasonal residents may have different views than permanent residents concerning the goals of public land management, they need to be involved through public meetings, surveys, and the variety of other collaborative techniques used to include stakeholders in collaborative management.

But as natural resources management policy becomes increasingly collaborative, it is encouraging that we find common ground among the diverse residents and seasonal homeowners of natural amenity communities in the Pine Barrens. The influx of seasonal homeowners as part-time residents, and for some later as retirees, may not be as disruptive as the community literature suggests. That is, the "culture clash" between urban seasonal homeowners and rural permanent residents does not appear to be as dramatic in our findings as one might expect, especially in terms of attitudes toward natural resources management.

The expression of common attitudes toward many aspects of public lands management holds promise for communities shifting to a consumption landscape. This has important implications for public land managers in many areas including the Intermountain West, northern New England, Blue Ridge Mountains, and the Ozarks. Public lands play linchpin roles in these landscapes and are associated with amenity-led development. Future studies of seasonal residents in these and other regions need to explore local beliefs and attitudes toward public land management. We find that in the natural amenity-rich Pine Barrens, contrary to public perception and scholarly expectations, broad public support for growth management and general agreement on resource management goals exists. The agreement and shared priorities of our Pine Barrens residents suggests residents in other amenity areas may also share values and management goals for their neighboring public lands. If this is the case, collaborative management will be more fruitful and successful for public land managers.

Community-based Resource Management

A second new paradigm of natural resource management—community-based management—has recently risen to prominence. Proponents of community-based resource management advocate a significant rethinking of conventional management (Grove and Burch 1997; Hviding and Baines 1994). Rather than a model of national public management or insular private management, community-based management builds upon the belief that communities within and around natural resources are the actors best equipped to manage them. This is distinct from collaborative management discussed above, because rather than public managers simply cooperating with community members, community-based management involves turning management of natural resources partly or entirely over to community members. Recognizing the importance of experiential knowledge, community-based management projects such as the Flathead Forestry Project in Montana (Daly 2003) and the Sino Forestry–Leadership Program in China (Burch 2007) have allowed community members to set their own use and management priorities for their natural resources. In Wisconsin, Pine Barrens residents are experimenting with community-based management by working with county and federal officials to connect private and public lands to create a connected land corridor for migrating species such as wolves and elk.

As the model of community-based resource management continues to spread, however, it becomes important to engage critically with the core concept of community. Too often, community-based resource management is extolled with little consideration of what defines a community (Flint, Luloff, and Finley 2008). In this vein, understanding the common priorities and goals of community members in amenity areas offers promise. The shared values and high levels of community attachment found in common between seasonal and permanent residents supports a community-based model that involves interactive, diverse communities. For example, Pine Barrens community members supported a mixed-use understanding of their forests and public lands, an understanding of natural resources that complements the community-based management model. The strong community attachment and shared ideology of community members also bodes well for the potential success of community-based management approaches. Such agreements offer confidence to those advocating community-based resource management in the United States. However, advocates of community-based management need to incorporate seasonal residents into their conception of community. As with nonresident business leaders, often ignored since they lacked ties to the community, seasonal residents should be seen as potential assets for community-based management. Like the nonresident business leaders, seasonal residents bring diversity, skills, and useful knowledge to these amenity communities.

Recognizing Population Diversity within Rural Communities

We have emphasized throughout our story the changing rural landscape of the Pine Barrens and the changing composition of the population living there. Migration is clearly an important aspect of change in rural America. Our study offers insights into some community impacts related to the growth and change affecting the nation's rural communities. New migrants in our study area actually bridge the gap between seasonal and permanent residents, and the much discussed culture clash between long-term residents and newcomers has lost some relevance. As exurbanization and natural amenity-led migration continue, general agreement of community members about development and management priorities offers hope. Seasonal residents bring more than social divides and tourist attitudes to their new communities; they may also bring social capital that can contribute to community well-being.

As rural amenity communities continue to change and grow, reflecting the needs of new migrants, seasonal residents, and long-term residents, it is essential for community members and those interested in planning to better understand the factors affecting community engagement. Rural America's natural amenity-rich areas are growing and changing at an astounding pace. With new seasonal developments being built and new business and recreational expansion, such communities struggle to maintain a precarious balance between prosperity and overdevelopment. Every zoning meeting can be a struggle, and long-term strategic planning is constantly in flux.

The residents of natural amenity-rich areas must actively address the economic, social, and environmental impacts of recreational and seasonal development as they deal with the past, present, and future of their communities. These communities' futures depend upon decisions made to balance potentially conflicting interests—the desire for growth with the demand for environmental protection, the desire to protect struggling agriculture with the call for economic diversification.

The apparent agreement between seasonal homeowners and permanent residents on many development goals and policies emphasizes the importance of social cohesion and an agreed-upon role for seasonal homeowners in local decision making. Reaching consensus on the status of seasonal homeowners may be at least as important as reaching agreement on a particular issue such as land-use planning. Until the members of such communities can agree upon the role of seasonal homeowners, it may be difficult for communities to negotiate differences about the substantive issues they face. However, as planning and development processes become more collaborative, seasonal residents can become better integrated into them. Local officials, planners, and citizens need to engage this growing population, break free of negative expectations, and be open to the possibility of positive integration and impacts of seasonal residents. Our findings suggest seasonal residents share many of the same attitudes and goals for development and growth management and have the potential to be an asset for planners and community members.

The general consensus and shared priorities between seasonal and permanent residents we find in the Pine Barrens suggests that social and cultural divides between the populations may not be as wide as often assumed. However, there may be some natural amenity-rich areas in which this gap may be more difficult to bridge. There are unique features of our study area, such as the high number of seasonal residents with family ties in the area and extensive prior contact with communities that are uncommon in many other natural amenity regions. The relatively affordable prices of land and homes also means that the income and education gaps between seasonal and permanent residents is not as wide in northwestern Wisconsin as in areas such as the Intermountain West or the southeastern United States. Further studies are needed to determine whether shared priorities are found in other regions, but our findings would suggest that pockets of community members—like seasonal residents who have extensive prior contact with the area or permanent residents who used to be seasonal residents—may serve as important potential bridges between different populations.

The Dynamic Nature of People and Places: A Final Note

Numerous studies mentioned throughout this book have documented the macro-demographic changes occurring in rural America as they shift from production to consumption landscapes. Our findings in northwestern Wisconsin and Burnett and Washburn Counties are consistent with national trends. Few rural communities maintain their traditional dependence upon extraction-based industries such as agriculture, mining, and timber. Instead they exhibit a variety of different development trajectories. For natural amenity-rich rural areas like northern Wisconsin, one of the most prevalent development paths has been a shift toward tourism and recreation-based economies.

Our examination explored community attachment, local social ties to friends and family, community civic participation, and management attitudes of both seasonal and permanent residents. We found several significant insights that enriched the understanding of amenity communities and the ways seasonal homeowners are integrated into them. Our analysis confirmed seasonal homeowners related to their host communities differently from permanent residents. As important as the variables that did affect attachment and engagement of seasonal residents were those that did not: in our statistical models, higher income, education, and seasonal homeowners' urban residence failed to have the comprehensive negative impact often assumed. This supports other recent studies that question these conventional community assumptions (Matarrita-Cascante and Luloff 2008). However, increasing the total number of days spent at their second home annually offered a consistent positive impact on the community engagement of seasonal homeowners.

We also demonstrated, in contrast to many assumptions, that a sub-population of seasonal homeowners was very involved in Pine Barrens community and civic affairs. They were members of community groups, volunteered in support of their community, and were active in local meetings and politics. Seasonal homeowners had significantly more friendship, family, and neighbor ties with permanent residents than vice versa and were surprisingly connected with and attached to their Pine Barrens communities. Among permanent residents, those who owned waterfront property and were wealthier bridged the gap and established more ties to seasonal residents than their peers. By analyzing the community engagement of this second-home area, we emerged with a better understanding of how seasonal homeownership is reshaping the social networks of rural America. We also found seasonal homeowners shared many of the same attitudes and values toward natural resource management, planning, and development as permanent residents. Instead of the "culture clash" and disagreement between seasonal and permanent residents often proffered, we found many shared values and common priorities.

People, culture, and the biophysical characteristics of natural resources shape patterns on the land. Migration to the countryside is changing the social fabric of rural space and nature as we know it. Placing our discussions of natural amenity regions within a rural sociological framework helps to emphasize the inherent connections between human community and natural environment. Although rarely framed as such, these stories of nonmetropolitan population change in the twenty-first century countryside are the contemporary equivalents of Landis's (1931) study of mining towns and Maher, Townsend, and Sanderson's (1934) analysis of New York farming practices.

Appendix A

In order to test the validity of using this additive scale for affectual community, we first analyzed the internal consistency of the scale using Cronbach's alpha.[1] The resulting additive variable then accounted for virtually 100 percent of the variation among the four variables and had a Cronbach's alpha score of 0.819. To further confirm the validity of the scale, we performed principal components factor analysis to determine if the variables loaded on a single factor and if their weights were approximately even on that factor.[2] The factor analysis of affectual attachment variables indicates that they load strongly and evenly onto a single factor. Given the high alpha score, the strong single-factor loading supports the assumption that these six variables actually measure a single underlying concept. The even loading of the variables indicates that the four variables are weighted evenly in the data set and supports the appropriateness of the additive scale.

The model for affectual community attachment required a particularly high level of model testing. First, we examined the dependent variable of community attachment and a histogram to determine that the variable was highly skewed to the left and not normal. The skewness and kurtosis test

1. Cronbach's alpha represents the proportion of the total variance of the scale that is explained by the variance of each component. A higher alpha indicates that the variables included in the scale are in fact measuring the same underlying concept.

2. Factor analysis determines a series of factors that best account for the combined variance of a series of variables. A high Eigenvalue indicates that the variables in a factor are measuring the same underlying concept, while the factor loadings indicate the weight that a variable should receive in the creation of the factor if variation in response is taken into account.

(sktest in the statistical software package STATA) for normality indicated problems. Sktest tests for both skewness (asymmetry of distribution) and kurtosis (distribution around the mean). Higher skewness means that the distribution of a variable is abnormally concentrated toward one end of the distribution. Kurtosis is a measure of a probability distribution's peakedness or flatness in comparison to a normal distribution; higher kurtosis is an indication that the variance of the distribution is abnormally affected by a few observations with high variance. Graphically comparing the quantiles of affectual attachment against a normal distribution (qnorm in STATA) also indicated that the distribution was not normal, especially at the tails.

Once recognizing that the variable for affectual community attachment was abnormal, we then performed some common variable transformations in order to improve normality of the dependent variable. First we created first the natural log of the variable and then the square root and square of the variable. Out of these three transformations, the square root of community attachment most closely approached normality. The sktest confirms that it is approaching normality, although still highly skewed. The problem still lies with the lower tail of the distribution; however, the square root seems to be the most normal option available that still maintains a form that is reasonable to interpret for substantive findings. The seasonal residents had a substantially more normal distribution of the dependent variable than either the combined or permanent population. The square root transformation still improves the normality, however, and so was retained in the model.

Because of the large number of sociodemographic variables we ran a full model with all independent variables and then conducted analysis to find reduced models. To create reduced models we ran step-wise forward and backward regressions (significance levels of $p = 0.2$ to enter the model and $p = 0.2$ to remain in the model) in STATA. In general, each selection procedure identified identical significant variables. When the selection procedures did not retain identical variables we retained all variables identified by each selection procedure. We then reanalyzed the data with the reduced number of independent variables.

We also followed procedures recommended by Freund and Littell (2000) to test the robustness and fitness of our statistical models, including analysis of residual plots, transformation of dependent variables (for example, for analysis of the dependent variable "number of friends" for permanent residents we used a log transformation), and removal of outliers (see table A.1).

As an example, after examining the residual plots and partial correlation plots for the model for community attachment of permanent residents, out-lier points were identified using the residual command in SAS (a statistical software package) that produces studentized residuals and Cook's D statistics for each point (Agresti and Finlay 1996; Freund and Littell 2000). These points were then removed from the data set and analyses run again. The results were essentially identical, though former seasonal residence becomes weakly significant in the model with the outliers removed. Upon further examination of the outliers it became clear that the outliers were generally the extreme scores on the given variable. Similarly, for the analysis of the community attachment of seasonal homeowners, a review of the partial residual plot of the number of days spent at the seasonal home suggested that there were a number of outlier points. Examination of the outliers revealed that the outliers corresponded to individuals who spent either an extremely high or low number of days at the home. We moved all extreme points (fewer than ten days and greater than three hundred days spent at the home) and reran the analysis. Results were again essentially identical.

TABLE A.I. Affectual community attachment OLS regression results

	Combined		Permanent		Seasonal	
	Full model	Reduced	Full model	Reduced	Full model	Reduced
Seasonal residency	−0.216*	−0.215***	—	—	—	—
Duration of residency	0.002	0.002	0.004**	0.003**	−0.0004	—
Waterfront property	0.017	—	−0.015	—	0.047	0.048
Rural childhood	0.003	—	−0.004	—	−0.0005	—
Children in household	−0.037	—	0.0007	—	−0.077	—
Age	−0.025	—	−0.025	—	−0.020	—
Age-squared	0.0003	0.00002*	0.0003	0.00003**	0.0002	—
Education	−0.019	—	−0.026	—	0.004	—
Male	−0.006	—	−0.081	—	0.065	—
Income	0.005	—	0.008	−0.008	—	—
Retired	−0.752	—	−0.840	—	0.511	—
Total days	—	—	—	—	0.002***	0.002***
Prior residence	—	—	—	—	0.133	—
Intention to relocate	—	—	—	—	0.129*	0.131*
Adjusted R-squared	0.1451***	0.1455***	0.0806***	0.0779***	0.1066***	0.0941***

SOURCE: Community and Natural Resources Survey 2002.

*$p < .05$; **$p \leq .01$; ***$p < .001$

Appendix B

TABLE B.I. OLS regression of number of friends, seasonal residents

	Full model	Reduced
Duration of residency	0.008	0.009*
Nonwaterfront property	0.094	0.103
Rural childhood	0.052	0.028
Children in household	−0.124	—
Age	0.035	—
Age-squared	−0.0004	—
Education	−0.055	−0.049
Male	0.047	—
Retired	−1.310	—
Total days	0.005***	0.004***
Prior residence	0.641	0.733***
Intention to relocate	0.059	—
Adjusted R-squared	0.1399***	0.1623***

SOURCE: Community and Natural Resources Survey 2002.

NOTE: Income had to be dropped from the models due to multicolinearity.
$^*p < .05; ^{**}p \leq .01; ^{***}p < .001$

TABLE B.2. Logistic regression of at least one community family tie, seasonal residents

	Full model		Reduced	
	ß	Wald	ß	Wald
Long-term residency	−0.048	0.03	—	—
Nonwaterfront property	−0.019	0.01	—	—
Rural childhood	0.010	0.02	—	—
Children in household	0.234	0.47	—	—
Age	−0.0003	0.00	—	—
Education	−0.228*	4.58*	−0.254**	8.68**
Male	0.013	0.00	—	—
Retired	−2.100	1.02	—	—
Total days	0.002	0.79	—	—
Prior residence	2.638**	11.16***	2.297***	13.38***
Intention to relocate	0.052	0.02	—	—
Wald Chi^2		23.21*		22.96***

SOURCE: Community and Natural Resources Survey 2002.

NOTE: Income had to be dropped from the models due to multicolinearity.

$^*p < .05$; $^{**}p \leq .01$; $^{***}p < .001$

TABLE B.3. Logistic regression of at least one friendship tie with permanent residents

	Full model		Reduced	
	ß	Wald	ß	Wald
Long-term residency	0.938**	7.73**	0.971**	10.29**
Nonwaterfront property	0.108	0.28	—	—
Rural childhood	0.340**	9.91**	0.360***	13.58***
Children in household	−0.161	0.18	—	—
Age	−0.006	0.08	—	—
Education	−0.087	0.51	—	—
Male	0.956**	7.01*	1.07**	9.96*
Ed income[a]	−0.089	2.57	−0.102*	4.93*
Retired	−0.862	0.14	—	—
Total days	0.010*	6.05*	0.009*	5.49*
Prior residence	0.700	0.72	—	—
Intention to relocate	0.608	2.39	0.769*	4.41*
Wald Chi²		39.15***		39.10***

SOURCE: Community and Natural Resources Survey 2002.

NOTE: Income had to be dropped from the models due to multicolinearity.

[a] The interaction between education and income.

$*p < .05; **p \leq .01; ***p < .001$

TABLE B.4. Logistic regression of at least one family tie with permanent
residents

	Full model		Reduced	
	ß	Wald	ß	Wald
Long-term residency	0.499	1.64	0.515	2.37
Nonwaterfront property	0.276	2.01	0.360*	4.35*
Rural childhood	0.167	2.75	0.115	1.54
Children	−0.172	0.17	—	—
Age	−0.022	0.79	—	—
Education	−0.170	1.73	−0.246*	
Male	0.215	0.27	—	—
Ed income[a]	−0.067	1.31	—	—
Age retired[b]	0.082*	3.71*	0.066*	3.70*
Retired	−5.178	3.52	−4.462*	3.61*
Total days	0.002	0.63	—	—
Prior residence	2.589***	14.08***	2.447***	16.61***
Intention to relocate	0.612	2.58	0.420	1.46
Wald Chi^2		44.80***		44.87***

SOURCE: Community and Natural Resources Survey 2002.

NOTE: Income had to be dropped from the models due to multicolinearity.

[a] The interaction between education and income.

[b] The interaction between age and retirement status.

*$p < .05$; **$p \leq .01$; ***$p < .001$

TABLE B.5. OLS regression of socializing with neighbors and permanent residents, seasonal residents

	Socializing with neighbors		Socializing with others	
	Full model	Reduced	Full model	Reduced
Duration of residency	−0.001	—	0.005	0.006
Nonwaterfront property	−0.168	—	0.077	0.106
Rural childhood	−0.010	—	0.043	0.058
Children	−0.355	−0.324	−0.106	—
Age	−0.087	—	−0.057	—
Age-squared	0.0009	—	0.0006	—
Ed income[a]	0.004	—	−0.040*	−0.038*
Education	−0.156	−0.081	0.028	—
Male	0.0551	0.460	0.060	—
Age retired[b]	−0.059	−0.008*	−0.022	−0.003
Retired	2.878	—	1.074	—
Total days	0.016***	0.015***	0.004**	0.004***
Prior residence	0.480	—	0.203	—
Intention to relocate	0.078	—	0.136	—
Adjusted R-squared	0.1707***	0.1622***	0.0882**	0.0975***

SOURCE: Community and Natural Resources Survey 2002.

NOTE: Income had to be dropped from the models due to multicolinearity.

[a] The interaction between education and income.

[b] The interaction between age and retirement status.

*$p < .05$; **$p \leq .01$; ***$p < .001$

TABLE B.6. OLS regression of number of friends, socializing with neighbors, and socializing with seasonal homeowners, permanent residents

	Number of friends		Socializing with neighbors		Socializing with others	
	Full model	Reduced	Full model	Reduced	Full model	Reduced
Duration of residency	0.014***	0.014***	-0.008	—	0.0007	—
Nonwaterfront property	-0.031	—	-0.561**	-0.559***	-0.293***	0.278***
Rural childhood	0.007	—	0.108	—	-0.054	-0.046
Children	0.233	0.140	-0.309	—	0.220	—
Age	-0.090*	-0.057	-0.218*	-0.160*	0.028	—
Age-squared	0.0008	0.0005	0.002	0.001*	-0.0002	—
Education	-0.060	-0.062	-0.037	—	-0.007	—
Male	0.190	0.179	0.180	—	0.107	—
Age retired[a]	-0.040	-0.026	-0.016	0.004	0.004	—
Retired	2.744*	1.922	1.188	—	-0.422	—
Adjusted R-squared	0.0802***	0.0971***	0.0425*	0.0560***	0.0785***	0.0989***

Source: Community and Natural Resources Survey 2002.

[a] The interaction between age and retirement status.

*p < .05; **p ≤ .01; ***p < .001

TABLE B.7. Logistic regression of seasonal residents belonging to at least one community organization

	Full model		Reduced	
	ß	Wald	ß	Wald
Long-term residency	0.303	0.94	—	—
Nonwaterfront property	−0.204	1.34	−0.277*	3.34
Rural childhood	−0.002	0.00	—	—
Children	0.0008	0.00	—	—
Age	−0.002	0.01	—	—
Education	0.182	2.91	0.161*	3.42
Male	0.251	0.58	—	—
Retired	0.260	0.02	—	—
Total days	0.015***	18.88***	0.010***	15.16***
Prior residence	0.403	0.61	—	—
Intention to relocate	−0.446	1.70	−0.278	0.90
Wald Chi^2		28.74**		23.75***

SOURCE: Community and Natural Resources Survey 2002.

$*p < .1$; $**p \leq .01$; $***p < .001$

Appendix C

SURVEY METHODOLOGY

Declining response rates to surveys, particularly for surveys of the general population, are generally accepted in the social sciences (Bradburn 1992; de Leeuw and De Heer 2002; Dillman et al. 1996; Smith 1995; Steeh 1981).[1] Indeed, a review of articles published in *Society and Natural Resources* from January 2001 to January 2003 (which reviewed Bright, Barro, and Burtz 2002; Carr and Halvorsen 2001; Connelly and Knuth 2002; Lauber, Anthony, and Knuth 2001; P. Nelson 2001; Vaske et al. 2001) finds response rates to mail surveys of the general U.S. population ranging from 41 percent to 68 percent, with a mean of 48 percent. Declining response rates are worrisome due to the potential impacts of nonresponse bias on the data collected, hampering attempts to draw inferences and analyze relationships. Our study illustrates that obtaining a high response rate for a self-administered survey of the general population is possible despite the downward trend. Employing an expanded version of Dillman's "tailored design method," we achieved an 82.8 percent response rate for a general population survey of landowners.

Our study further explores concerns about nonresponse bias by examining differences between early and late respondents in their demographic characteristics and attitudes toward natural resources management. Comparisons were made between respondents from the commonly adopted

1. An expanded version of this appendix was published in *Society and Natural Resources* (Clendenning, Field, and Jensen 2004). Reprinted with permission.

four-wave mailing recommended by Dillman's (1978, 2000) earlier work (early respondents) and those who responded after additional mailings that were employed for this study (late respondents). Despite a 70 percent response rate after four mailings, significant differences were detected between early and late respondents on a number of measures.

Survey Methodology

Previous research has shown that a number of factors influence response rates, both positively and negatively. Among the most influential positive factors are the number of contacts, visual presentation of the survey, personalization of correspondence with respondents, and financial incentives. In contrast, length of survey and surveys of the general population negatively affect response rates (see Dillman 1991, 2000; Heberlein and Baumgartner 1978). Our study shows that survey design and implementation that pay heed to these factors can achieve high response rates, even for a long survey of the general population. Our survey, eighteen pages in length, included 170 response items and took approximately twenty to twenty-five minutes to complete. Despite the length of the survey we achieved a response rate of 82.8 percent. We feel that this was a result of several key elements of our survey design and methodology, including a higher than usual number of mailings sent to late respondents.

Survey Design and Layout

Self-administered questionnaires place particular burdens on respondents when compared with other survey interview methods, making design a critical consideration. The general model of the interview process holds that a respondent first comprehends a question, retrieves the relevant information, makes a judgment, and concludes with a response (Jenkins and Dillman 1997). However, self-administered questionnaires place additional burdens on respondents. First, respondents must perceive the information. Then they must comprehend both the visual elements of the layout and the written elements of the survey. In addition, respondents must comprehend introductory materials, instructions contained in cover letters, and specialized instructions that occur throughout the survey. With this in mind, the visual elements of the survey must help guide respondents through the survey, reducing respondent burden and error, while verbal elements must present information and questions in a well-organized fashion (Jenkins and Dillman 1997). Poorly organized and presented surveys tend to increase respondent frustration, often leading to inaccurate responses or even refusals (Dillman 2000; Dillman, Sinclair, and Clark 1993; Dillman et al. 1996; Heberlein and Baumgartner 1978).

Our survey paid particular attention to six visual elements: location of and spacing between elements of the survey; the shape of questions and responses; size of fonts and images; brightness and shading in the survey; simplicity and regularity; and consistent figure-ground formatting (Dillman 1991, 2000). For example, individual questions and responses were enclosed in a box with light gray shading, making each question easily distinguishable from other questions. Questions, printed in a dark, bold font, were easily distinguished from responses. White spaces, easily identifiable against the gray background, were used for respondent answers. In addition, the survey was printed in a large font for ease of reading. While this increased the number of pages in the survey, it eased respondent burden in filling out the survey. Fewer items were included on each page of the survey, reinforcing the respondent's progress through the survey through page turning (Dillman 1991, 2000; Heberlein and Baumgartner 1978). Two versions of the survey were used, one for seasonal residents and one for permanent residents. Question and instruction wording were slightly modified for seasonal residents because many of the questions of our survey were pertinent to both their permanent residence and their recreational homes.

Cover Description

According to Dillman (1991, 2000), a memorable and retrievable cover design can help improve response rates. This increase in response rates has been attributed to improved recall of the survey when postcard reminders are sent. Our cover, a glossy color photograph of a pristine lake in northern Wisconsin, resonates with landowners and residents of the entire Lake States region, as "up north" is generally associated with pristine lakes, forests, and natural resources (see Northwest 2000; Wisconsin DNR 1996, 2000).

Distinctive Packaging

In an effort to distinguish the survey from other mail, the survey was sent in a large (ten by thirteen inches) windowed envelope with the color cover of the survey prominently displayed. The strategy was that unusual packaging and a distinctive survey cover that is seen through the envelope window may draw attention to the survey, reducing the chances of the survey being accidentally discarded or perceived as junk mail (Dillman 2000).

Survey Sampling Frame

We created a sample frame of all residential property owners inside the
Pine Barrens using property tax records. Using simple random sampling, a
sample of 800 households was drawn. Type of residence (seasonal or permanent) was then determined by the zip code of the property tax billing
address using Census 2000 tiger data files. Our sample consisted of 422 permanent residents and 378 seasonal residents, approximating the distribution of seasonal and permanent households in the population.

Implementing the Survey

A modified version of Dillman's Tailored Design Method (Dillman 2000)
was used to implement the survey. Instead of the typical four-wave mailing
we used seven total mailings: a pre-notification letter, the survey, a reminder
postcard, a replacement survey, two additional postcard reminders, and a
specially delivered third copy of the survey. We modified Dillman's method
by sending two additional postcard reminders and by using distinctive
packaging to display our cover.

   All mailings followed Dillman's (2000) recommendations to personalize
communication (letters and postcard were dated, personally addressed, and
hand-signed) and to take steps to add legitimacy and trust (university spon-
sorship of the research, use of university letterhead, provision of a toll-free
telephone number in case of questions). In addition, a $2 bill was enclosed
with the first survey sent to respondents. Providing respondents with a
tangible gift is critical in rewarding respondents and improving response
rates. Further, the $2 gift appeals to the strong social norm of reciprocity
that leads individuals to strive to repay favors freely given (see Gouldner
1960; Groves, Cialdini, and Couper 1992). Our seventh and final mailing, following the recommendations of Dillman (2000) and Heberlein and
Baumgartner (1978), was sent via a special mode of delivery: U.S. Postal
Service priority mail. This different and more expensive mode of delivery
adds legitimacy and perceived importance of the survey to the final non-
respondents to the survey (Dillman 2000).

Response Rates

Our final response rate was 82.8 percent, and return rates for seasonal residents and permanent residents were comparable, 85.4 percent and 80.4
percent, respectively. Examining the response rate over the course of the
mailings reveals that we achieved a high response rate of 63.4 percent by the

time the second survey was mailed and a 70 percent response rate after four mailings (see table C.1). While it is difficult to attribute the exact number of surveys returned to any particular mailing, it does appear as though the second survey and second postcard reversed the declining trend in response rates (see figure C.1). It is unclear whether the third postcard exhibited much influence on the final response rate. However, the third survey, sent priority mail, seemed to be quite effective. At the time of this mailing returns had dwindled to almost zero. Remarkably, over 28 percent of the outstanding surveys were returned during this mailing, the third highest rate for any single mailing. Together, the three extra mailings added close to 13 percent to our final response rate.

Comparing Costs

An obvious concern in implementing any study is the cost. One might reasonably ask whether the costs incurred when employing the methods described in this study are excessive in comparison to using the more standard four-wave method. An analysis of costs reveals that these methods are not exceedingly more expensive in obtaining the same number of respondents. Assuming a trade-off between a simplified survey with fewer mailings and lower response rate, we use the average response rate of 48 percent from recent general population surveys in the United States. Obtaining 653 respondents would then require a much larger sample of 1,356 households. One could make savings on each individual survey if we removed the color cover (a savings of approximately $1 per survey), changed the layout to cut the number of pages in half (reducing both printing costs and postage costs) and did not include a $2 incentive. However, much of the savings are lost in the added cost of printing and mailing 556 more surveys. Assuming a response rate of 40 percent at the time the fourth and final mailing is made, total costs of the survey exceed $9,100 (see table C.2). While this is considerably less than the $10,600 spent on our survey, the difference is less than one might expect. By focusing resources on improving response rates, increased per-survey costs are largely offset by requiring a smaller sample and by obtaining a large number of early respondents, reducing the number of replacement surveys mailed.

CONCLUSIONS AND IMPLICATIONS

Declining response rates and nonresponse bias continues to be a concern for survey research. This study illustrates that adopting and slightly modifying well-substantiated survey procedures can result in high response rates. Our methodology adhered to and modified survey procedures such as the number of contacts, the visual presentation of the survey, personalization of correspondence with respondents, and financial incentives. For example, we increased the total number of contacts from the commonly adopted four to seven. We have also extended the principle of the visual presentation of the survey by using a memorable cover to the survey and distinctive packaging. These steps helped distinguish the survey from other mail. These procedures, in concert with other effective and proven procedures such as postage-paid return envelopes, encouraged high response rates. Of further interest, our procedures do not appear to be dramatically more expensive than a more simplified four-wave mailing procedure. This is largely due to the increased sample size needed to obtain a similar number of respondents for the four-wave method.

In exploring the possible impacts of a lower response rate on nonresponse bias, our findings are consistent with recent findings (see Chen, Wei, and Syme 2003; Curtin, Presser, and Singer 2000). Demographic and attitudinal differences, while not dramatic, were found. Salience of the survey topic may have been an issue as late respondents held more neutral attitudes toward natural resource management issues. This appears to be more of an issue for seasonal respondents, as more differences were found between early and late seasonal respondents than between early and late permanent respondents. Differences detected between early and late respondents suggest that had our survey procedures stopped after four mailings, we might have made an inaccurate depiction of the population and might have inaccurately characterized some bivariate and multivariate relationships.

As the rural United States continues to undergo dramatic change and resource managers approach management from a more collaborative and community-based approach, public land managers and community planners need to know more about the people inhabiting and shaping the land around them. Including a more coherent characterization of people, organizational structure, and social relations on the land is essential to this understanding. A mail survey is an excellent tool for obtaining this kind of information, especially from nonresidents such as seasonal landowners. Nonresponse bias continues to be a concern; therefore we suggest that resources be focused on improving response rates. Our research demonstrates that requiring a smaller initial sample can largely offset added per-survey costs.

TABLE C.1. Survey response rates by mailing

Mailing	Number of outstanding surveys at time of mailing[a]	Number of surveys returned during the mailing	Percentage of outstanding surveys returned during the mailing	Overall response rate (%)
1st survey	789	264	33.50	33.5
1st postcard reminder	523	237	45.30	63.5
2nd survey	279	52	18.60	70.1
2nd postcard reminder	217	47	21.70	76.1
3rd postcard reminder	158	16	10.10	78.1
3rd survey, priority mail	129	37	28.70	82.8

SOURCE: Clendenning, Field, and Jensen 2004.

[a] The number of outstanding surveys did not include undeliverable surveys or refusals. Refusals were blank surveys returned by members of the sample.

TABLE C.2. Estimated cost of 4-wave mailing

Item	Item cost ($)	Number of outstanding surveys at time of mailing	Total costs ($)
Pre-notification letter, envelope, and postage	0.70	1,356	949.20
Survey (printing)	1.00	1,356	1,356.00
Survey postage, cover letter, labels, envelopes, processing	2.39	1,356	3,240.84
Postcard (printing, processing, and postage)	0.60	1,356	813.60
2nd survey (printing)	1.00	814	814.00
2nd survey postage, cover letter, labels, envelopes, processing	2.39	814	1,945.46
Total cost			9,119.10

SOURCE: Clendenning, Field, and Jensen 2004.

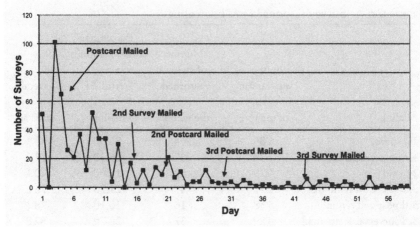

FIGURE C.I. Daily survey returns (Clendenning, Field, and Jensen 2004)

Works Cited

Agresti, A., and B. Finlay. 1997. *Statistical Methods for the Social Sciences*. Upper Saddle River, NJ: Prentice Hall.

Albarre, G. 1977. "Second Homes and Conservation in Southern Belgium." In Coppock 1977b, 139–46.

Allen, L. R., P. Long, R. P. Perdue, and S. Kieselbach. 1988. "The Impact of Tourism on Residents' Perceptions of Community Life." *Journal of Travel Research* 27 (1): 16–21.

American Society of Planning Officials. 1976. *Subdividing Rural America: Impacts of Recreational Lot and Second Home Development*. Washington, DC: Council on Environmental Quality.

Audirac, I. 1999. "Unsettled Views about the Fringe: Rural-Urban or Urban-Rural Frontiers?" In *Contested Countryside: The Rural Urban Fringe in North America*, edited by O. J. Furuseth, and Mark B. Lapping, 7–32. Brookfield, VT: Ashgate.

Bawden, T. 1997. "The Northwoods: Back to Nature?" In *Wisconsin Land and Life*, edited by R. C. Ostergren and T. R. Vale, 450–69. Madison: University of Wisconsin Press.

Beale, C. L., and K. M. Johnson. 1998. "The Identification of Recreational Counties in Nonmetropolitan Areas of the USA." *Population Research and Policy Review* 17:37–53.

Beckley, T. M. 1996. "Pluralism by Default: Community Power in a Paper Mill Town." *Forest Science* 42 (1): 35–45.

Bielckus, C. L. 1977. "Second Homes in Scandinavia." In Coppock 1977b, 35–36.

Beyers, W., and P. Nelson. 2000. "Contemporary Development Forces in the Nonmetropolitan West: New Insights from Rapidly Growing Communities." *Journal of Rural Studies* 16 (4): 459–74.

Blahna, D. J. 1990. "Social Bases for Resource Conflicts in Areas of Reverse Migration." In *Community and Forestry: Continuities in the Sociology of Natural Resources,* edited by R. G. Lee, D. R. Field, and W. R. Burch Jr., 159–78. Boulder, CO: Westview Press.

Bliss, J. C., T. L. Walkingstick, and C. Bailey. 1998. "Development or Dependency? Sustaining Alabama's Forest Communities." *Journal of Forestry* 96 (3): 24–30.

Bostic, R. W., and B. J. Surette. 2001. "Have the Doors Opened Wider? Trends in Homeownership Rates by Race and Income." *Journal of Real Estate Finance and Economics* 23 (3): 411–34.

Boyle, P., and K. Halfacree, eds. *Migration into Rural Areas: Theories and Issues*. New York: John Wiley and Sons.

Bradburn, N. M. 1992. "Presidential Address: A Response to the Non-Response Problem." *Public Opinion Quarterly* 56:391–98.

Brick, P., D. Snow, and S. Van de Wetering, eds. 2001. *Across the Great Divide: Explorations in Collaborative Conservation and the American West*. Washington, DC: Island Press.

Bright, A. D., S. C. Barro, and R. T. Burtz. 2002. "Public Attitudes towards Ecological Restoration in the Chicago Metropolitan Region." *Society and Natural Resources* 15 (9): 763–86.

Brown, D. L., G. V. Fuguitt, T. B. Heaton, and S. Waseem. 1997. "Continuities in Size of Place Preference, 1972–1992." *Rural Sociology* 62 (4): 408–28.

Burch, W. R. 2007. "Looking Forward, Community Based Forestry." Paper presented at the annual meeting of the Rural Sociological Society, Santa Clara, CA, August 2–5.

Carr, D. S., and K. E. Halvorsen. 2001. "An Evaluation of Three Democratic, Community-Based Approaches to Citizen Participation: Surveys, Conversations with Community Groups, and Community Dinners." *Society and Natural Resources* 14 (2): 107–26.

Chen, R., L. Wei, and P. D. Syme. 2003. "Comparison of Early and Delayed Respondents to a Postal Health Survey: A Questionnaire Study of Personality Traits and Neuropsychological Symptoms." *European Journal of Epidemiology* 18 (3): 195–202.

Christensen, N. L., A. M. Bartuska, J. H. Brown, S. Carpenter, C. D'Antonio, R. Francis, J. F. Franklin, J. A. MacMahon, R. F. Noss, D. J. Parsons, C. H. Peterson, M. G. Turner, and R. G. Woodmansee. 1996. "The Report of the Ecological Society of America Committee on the Scientific Basis for Ecosystem Management." *Ecological Applications* 6 (3): 665–91.

Chubb, M. 1989. "Tourism Patterns and Determinants in the Great Lakes Region: Populations, Resources, Roads, and Perceptions." *GeoJournal* 19 (3): 297–302.

Chubb, M., and H. Chubb. 1981. *One Third of Our Time*. New York: John Wiley and Sons.

Clendenning, G. 2004. "Seasonal Homeowners, Community Change, and Natural Resources Management in the Amenity-Rich Exurbs of the Wisconsin Pine Barrens." PhD diss., University of Wisconsin–Madison.

Clendenning, G., and D. R. Field. 2005. "Seasonal Residents: Members of Community or Part of the Scenery?" In *Amenities and Rural Development: Theory,*

Methods, and Public Policy, edited by Gary Paul Green, Steven C. Deller, and David W. Marcoullier, 216–37. Northampton, MA: Edward Elgar.

Clendenning, G., D. R. Field, and D. A. Jensen. 2004. "A Survey of Seasonal and Permanent Landowners in Wisconsin's Northwoods: Following Dillman and Then Some." *Society and Natural Resources* 17 (5): 431–42.

Clout, H. D. 1977. "Residences Secondaires in France." In Coppock 1977b, 47–62.

Cockerham, W. C., and A. L. Belvins Jr. 1977. "Attitudes towards Land-Use Planning and Controlled Population Growth in Jackson Hole." *Journal of Community Development Society* 8 (1): 62–73.

Community and Natural Resources Survey. 2002. "A Survey of Seasonal and Permanent Landowners in Wisconsin's Northwoods." Data collected June–July.

Connelly, N. A., and B. A. Knuth. 2002. "Using the Coorientation Model to Compare Community Leaders' and Local Residents' Views about Hudson River Ecosystem Restoration." *Society and Natural Resources* 15 (10): 933–48.

Coppock, J. T. 1977a. "The Impact of Second Homes: Social Implications of Second Homes in Mid and North Wales." In Coppock 1977b, 147–54.

——— ed. 1977b. *Second Homes: Curse or Blessing?* New York: Pergamon Press.

———. 1977c. "Second Homes in Perspective." In Coppock 1977b, 1–16.

Cortner, H. J., and M. A. Moote. 1999. *Politics of Ecosystem Management.* Washington, DC: Island Press.

Cox, K. R., and A. Mair. 1988. "Locality and Community in the Politics of Local Economic Development." *Annals of the Association of American Geographers* 78 (2): 307–25.

Cromartie, J. B. 1998. "Net Migration in the Great Plains Increasingly Linked to Natural Amenities and Suburbanization." *Rural Development Perspectives* 13 (1): 27–34.

Crownhart, M. 1965. *Strolling through a Century: The Story of Grantsburg, Burnett County, Wisconsin from 1865–1965.* Prepared with the Grantsburg Centennial Committee. Grantsburg, WI: Crownhart Printing.

Cuba, L. J. 1989. "Retiring in Vacationland." *Generations* 13 (1): 63–67.

Cuba, L. J., and D. H. Hummon. 1993. "Constructing a Sense of Home: Place Affiliation and Migration across the Life Cycle." *Sociological Forum* 8 (4): 547–71.

Curtin, R., S. Presser, and E. Singer. 2000. "The Effects of Response Rate Changes on the Index of Consumer Sentiment." *Public Opinion Quarterly* 64:413–28.

Daly, M. 2003. "Community-Based Forestry Takes Root in the U.S." *Grist.* Retrieved from http://www.grist.org/article/daly-forest.

Daniels, M. (1934) 1992. Personal correspondence. In *Iron River, Wisconsin Centennial, 1892–1992,* 21–29. Iron River, WI: Book Committee.

Daniels, S. E., and G. B. Walker. 1995. "Managing Local Environmental Conflict amidst National Controversy." *International Journal of Conflict Management* 6 (3): 290–311.

Daniels, T. L. 1999. *When City and Country Collide: Managing Growth in the Metropolitan Fringe.* Washington, DC: Island Press.

Davis, M. 1997. "An Empire in Waiting: Northern Wisconsin's Lake Country, 1880–1940." PhD diss., University of Wisconsin–Madison.

Dearden, P. 1983. "Tourism and the Resource Base." *Tourism in Canada: Selected Issues and Options*, edited by Peter E. Murphy, 75–93. Western Geographical Series 21. Victoria, BC: University of Victoria.

de Leeuw, Edith, and Wim de Heer. 2002. "Trends in Household Survey Nonresponse: A Longitudinal and International Comparison." In *Survey Nonresponse*, edited by R. M. Groves, D. A. Dillman, J. L. Eltinge, and R. J. A. Little, 41–54. New York: John Wiley and Sons.

Deller, S. C., D. W. Marcouiller, and G. P. Green. 1997. "Recreational Housing and Local Government Finance." *Annals of Tourism Research* 24 (3): 687–705.

Dillman, D. A. 1978. *Mail and Telephone Surveys: The Total Design Method*. New York: John Wiley and Sons.

———. 1991. "Design and Administration of Mail Surveys." *Annual Review of Sociology* 17:225–49.

———. 2000. *Mail and Internet Surveys: The Tailored Design Method*. New York: John Wiley and Sons.

Dillman, D. A., M. Sinclair, and J. R. Clark. 1993. "Effects of Questionnaire Length, Respondent-Friendly Design, and a Difficult Question on Response Rates for Occupant-Addressed Census Mail Surveys." *Public Opinion Quarterly* 57:289–304.

Dillman, D. A., E. Singer, J. R. Clark, and J. B. Treat. 1996. "Effects of Benefits Appeals, Mandatory Appeals, and Variations in Statements of Confidentiality on Completion Rates for Census Questionnaires." *Public Opinion Quarterly* 60:376–89.

Dower, M. 1977. "Planning Aspects of Second Homes." In Coppock 1977b, 155–64.

Doxey, G. V. 1975. "A Causation Theory of Visitor-Resident Irritants: Methodology and Research Inferences." In *The Impact of Tourism: Sixth Annual Conference Proceedings of the Travel Research Association*, 195–98. San Diego: Travel Research Association.

Dubbink, D. 1984. "I'll Have My Town Medium Rural, Please." *Journal of the American Planning Association* 50 (4): 406–18.

Eastwood, D. A., and R. W. Carter. 1981. "The Irish Dune Consumer." *Journal of Leisure Research* 13 (4): 273–81.

Egan, A. F., and A. E. Luloff. 2000. "The Exurbanization of America's Forests." *Journal of Forestry* 98 (3): 26–30.

Elo, I. T., and C. L. Beale. 1983. *Natural Resources and Poverty: An Overview*. Washington DC: Resources for the Future.

Endter-Wada, J., D. Blahna, R. S. Krannich, and M. Brunson. 1998. "A Framework for Understanding Social Science Contributions to Ecosystem Management." *Ecological Applications* 8 (3): 891–904.

Field, D. R., and W. R. Burch Jr. 1988. *Rural Sociology and the Environment*. Middleton, WI: Social Ecology Press.

Fine, Isadore Victor, and E. E. Werner. 1966. "Private Cottages in Wisconsin." In *Private Seasonal Housing in Wisconsin*, n.p. Madison: Wisconsin Department of Resource Development.

Fischer, C. S. 1982. *To Dwell among Friends*. Chicago: University of Chicago Press.

———. 1984. *The Urban Experience*. San Diego: Harcourt Brace Jovanovich.

Fischer, C. S., C. A. Stueve, K. Gerson, L. M. Jones, and M. Baldassare. 1977. *Networks and Places: Social Relations in the Urban Setting*. New York: Free Press.

Fishman, R. 1990. "Megalopolis Unbound." *Wilson Quarterly* 14 (1): 25–47.

Fliegel, F. C., A. J. Sofranko, and N. Glasgow. 1981. "Population Growth in Rural Areas and Sentiments of the New Migrants toward Further Growth." *Rural Sociology* 46 (3): 411–29.

Flint, C. G., A. E. Luloff, and J. C. Finley. 2008. "Where Is 'Community' in Community-Based Forestry?" *Society and Natural Resources* 21 (6): 526–37.

Force, J. E., G. E. Machlis, and L. Zhang. 2000. "The Engines of Change in Resource Dependent Communities." *Forest Science* 46 (3): 410–22.

Fortmann, L., J. Kusel, M. Olson, and C. Danks. 1991. "Study 1: The Effects of Forest Control and Use on County Well-Being." In *Well-Being in Forest Dependent Communities*, edited by J. Kusel and L. Fortmann, 49–75. Sacramento, CA: Forest and Rangeland Resources Assessment Program.

Freudenburg, W. R. 1986. "The Density of Acquaintanceship: An Overlooked Variable in Community Research?" *American Journal of Sociology* 92 (1): 27–63.

———. 1992. "Addictive Economies: Extractive Industries and Vulnerable Localities in a Changing World Economy." *Rural Sociology* 57 (3): 305–32.

Freund, R. J., and R. C. Littell. 2000. *SAS System for Regression*. Cary, NC: SAS.

Frey, W. H., and K. M. Johnson. 1998. "Concentrated Immigration, Restructuring and the 'Selective' Deconcentration of the United States Population." In Boyle and Halfacre, *Migration into Rural Areas*, 79–106.

Frey, W. H., and A. Speare. 1992. "The Revival of Metropolitan Population-Growth in the United States—An Assessment of Findings from the 1990 Census." *Population and Development Review* 18 (1): 129–46.

Fuguitt, G. 1985. "The Nonmetropolitan Population Turnaround." *Annual Review of Sociology* 11:259–80.

Gartner, W. 1987. "Environmental Impacts of Recreational Home Developments." *Annals of Tourism Research* 14 (1): 38–57.

Gates, P. W. (1943) 1965. *The Wisconsin Pine Lands of Cornell University: A Study in Land Policy and Absentee Ownership*. Ithaca, NY: Cornell University Press. Reprint, Madison: State Historical Society of Wisconsin.

Girard, T. C., and W. C. Gartner. 1993. "Second Home Second View: Host Community Perceptions." *Annals of Tourism Research* 20 (4): 685–700.

Gobster, P. H., and M. G. Rickenbach. 2004. "Private Forestland Parcelization and Development in Wisconsin's Northwoods: Perceptions of Resource-Oriented Stakeholders." *Landscape and Urban Planning* 69 (2/3): 165–82.

Gonen, A. 1981. "Tourism and Coastal Settlement Processes in the Mediterranean Region." *Ekistics* 48 (290): 378–81.

Goudy, W. J. 1982. "Further Consideration of Indicators of Community Attachment." *Social Indicators Research* 11:181–92.

———. 1990. "Community Attachment in a Rural Region." *Rural Sociology* 55 (2): 178–98.

Gough, R. 1997. *Farming the Cutover: A Social History of Northern Wisconsin, 1900–1940.* Lawrence: University Press of Kansas.

Gouldner, A. 1960. "The Norm of Reciprocity." *American Sociological Review* 25 (2): 161–78.

Graber, E. E. 1974. "Newcomers and Oldtimers: Growth and Change in a Mountain Town." *Rural Sociology* 39 (4): 504–13.

Grantsburg Chamber of Commerce. 2008. "Grantsburg, Wisconsin." Retrieved from http://www.grantsburgwi.com/.

Green, G. P., and G. Clendenning. 2003. "Second Homes." In *Encyclopedia of Community: From the Village to the Virtual World*, edited by Karen Christensen and David Levinson, 1209–12. Thousand Oaks, CA: Sage.

Green, G. P., D. Marcouiller, S. Deller, D. Erkkila, and N. Sumathi. 1996. "Local Dependency, Land Use Attitudes, and Economic Development: Comparisons between Seasonal and Permanent Residents." *Rural Sociology* 61 (3): 227–45.

Greider, T., and L. Garkovich. 1994. "Landscapes: The Social Construction of Nature and the Environment." *Rural Sociology* 59 (1): 1–24.

Groth, P. E. 1997. "Frameworks for Cultural Landscape Study." In *Understanding Ordinary Landscapes*, edited by P. E. Groth and T. W. Bressi, 1–22. New Haven, CT: Yale University Press.

Groth, P. E., and T. W. Bressi, eds. 1997. *Understanding Ordinary Landscapes.* New Haven, CT: Yale University Press.

Grove, J. M, and W. R. Burch. 1997. "A Social Ecology Approach and Applications of Urban Ecosystem and Landscape Analyses: A Case Study of Baltimore, Maryland." *Urban Ecosystems* 1 (4): 259–75.

Groves, R. M., R. Cialdini, and M. P. Couper. 1992. "Understanding the Decision to Participate in a Survey." *Public Opinion Quarterly* 56:475–95.

Groves, T. 1986. "Management of Aquatic Plants in Small Inland Lakes in Michigan." *Michigan Riparian: A Magazine for Waterfront Property Owners*, February, 18–20.

Grumbine, E. R. 1994. "What Is Ecosystem Management?" *Conservation Biology* 8 (1): 27–38.

Gustafson, P. 2002. "Tourism and Seasonal Retirement Migration." *Annals of Tourism Research* 29 (4): 899–918.

———. 2006. "Place Attachment and Mobility." In *Multiple Dwelling and Tourism: Negotiating Place, Home and Identity*, edited by Norman McIntyre, Daniel R. Williams, and Kevin E. McHugh, 17–31. Cambridge, MA: CABI.

Halfacree, K. 1997. "Contrasting Roles for the Post-Productivist Countryside." In *Contested Countryside Cultures*, edited by Paul Cloke and J. Little, 70–93. New York: Routledge.

Halfacree, K., and P. Boyle. 1998. "Migration, Rurality and the Post-Productivist Countryside." In Boyle and Halfacre, *Migration into Rural Areas*, 1–20.

Halseth, G. 1998. *Cottage Country in Transition*. Montreal: McGill-Queen's University Press.

Hammer, R. B., S. I. Stewart, T. J. Hawbaker, and V. C. Radeloff. 2009. "Housing Growth, Forests, and Public Lands in Northern Wisconsin from 1940 to 2000." *Journal of Environmental Management* 90:2690–98.

Hay, R. 1998. "Sense of Place in Developmental Context." *Journal of Environmental Psychology* 18 (1): 5–29.

Haynes, R. 2003. "Economic Analysis in Support of Broad Scale Land Management Strategies." *Forest Policy and Economics* 5 (4): 361–71.

Healey, P. 1997. *Collaborative Planning: Shaping Places in Fragmented Societies*. London, Macmillan.

Heberlein, T. A., and R. Baumgartner. 1978. "Factors Affecting Response Rates to Mailed Questionnaires: A Quantitative Analysis of the Published Literature." *American Sociological Review* 43 (4): 447–62.

Henshal, J. D. 1977. "Second Homes in the Caribbean." In Coppock 1977b, 75–84.

Hummon, D. 1992. "Community Attachment: Local Sentiment and Sense of Place." In *Place Attachment*, edited by Irwin Altman and Setha M. Low, 253–78. New York: Plenum Press.

Humphries, C. R. 1986. "Innovative Condominium Development for Northern Michigan Riparian Wetlands." Agriculture and Natural Resource Program, Department of Resource Development, Michigan State University, East Lansing, MI.

Hunter, A. 1974. *Symbolic Communities: The Persistence and Change of Chicago's Local Communities*. Chicago: University of Chicago Press.

———. 1975. "The Loss of Community: An Empirical Test through Replication." *American Sociological Review* 40 (5): 537–52.

———. 1978. "Persistence of Local Sentiments in Mass Society." In *Handbook of Contemporary Urban Life*, edited by David Street, 133–62. San Francisco: Jossey-Bass.

Hviding, E., and G. B. K. Baines. 1994. "Community-Based Fisheries Management, Tradition and the Challenges of Development in Marovo, Solomon Islands." *Development and Change* 25 (1): 13–39.

Iron River Chamber of Commerce. 2008. "Vacation in Iron River, Wisconsin!" Retrieved from http://www.iracc.com/.

Iron River Times. (1892) 1992. In *Iron River, Wisconsin Centennial, 1892–1992*. Iron River, WI: Book Committee.

Iron River, Wisconsin Centennial, 1892–1992. 1992. Iron River, WI: Book Committee.

Jaakson, R. 1986. "Second-Home Domestic Tourism." *Annals of Tourism Research* 13 (3): 367–91.

Jackson, S. 1974. "Environmental Considerations: Regulatory Aspects." In *Recreational Land Development: The Second Home Bonanza*, edited by Peter J. Lane, 17–28. New York: Practising Law Institute.

Jarvis, T. D. 2000. "The Responsibility of National Parks in Rural Development." In *National Parks and Rural Development: Practice and Policy in the United States*, edited by Gary E. Machlis and Donald R. Field, 219–30. Washington, DC: Island Press.

Jenkins, C., and D. Dillman. 1997. "Towards a Theory of Self-Administered Questionnaire Design." In *Survey Measurement and Process Quality*, edited by L. Lyberg, P. Biemer, M. Collins, L. Decker, E. de Leeuw, C. Dippo, N. Schwarz, and D. Trewin, 165–96. New York: Wiley-Interscience.

Jensen, D. A., and D. R. Field. 2004. "Landowner Attitudes and Perceptions toward Planning and Growth in Northwest Wisconsin: Implications for Managing Growth and Development in a Natural Amenity-Rich Landscape." Paper presented at Amenities and Rural Development Conference, University of Wisconsin–Madison, June 18–19.

Johnson, K. M. 1999. "The Rural Rebound." *Population Reference Bureau Reports on America* 1 (3): 1–19.

Johnson, K. M., and C. L. Beale. 2002. "Nonmetro Recreation Counties: Their Identification and Rapid Growth." *Rural America* 17 (4): 12–19.

Johnson, K. M., and G. Fuguitt. 2000. "Continuity and Change in Rural Migration Patterns, 1950–1995." *Rural Sociology* 65 (1): 27–49.

Jordan, J. W. 1980. "The Summer People and the Natives: Some Effects of Tourism in a Vermont Vacation Village." *Annals of Tourism Research* 7 (1): 34–55.

Kaltenborn, B. 1997. "Recreation Homes in Natural Settings: Factors Affecting Place Attachment." *Norwegian Journal of Geography* 51 (4): 187–98.

Kasarda, J. D., and M. Janowitz. 1974. "Community Attachment in Mass Society." *American Sociological Review* 39:328–39.

Kates, J. 2001. *Planning a Wilderness: Regenerating the Great Lakes Cutover Region*. Minneapolis: University of Minnesota Press.

Kaufman, H. F., and L. C. Kaufman. 1946. *Toward the Stabilization and Enrichment of a Forest Community: The Montana Study*. Missoula: University of Montana.

Kemmis, D. 1990. *Community and the Politics of Place*. Norman: University of Oklahoma Press.

Klessig, L. L. 1973. *Recreational Property Owners and Their Institutional Alternatives for Resource Protection: The Case of Wisconsin Lakes*. Madison, WI: Inland Lake Demonstration Project.

Kolb, J. H., and R. A. Polson. 1933. *Trends in Town-Country Relations*. Agricultural Research Bulletin 117. Madison: University of Wisconsin, Agricultural Experiment Station.

Krannich, R. S., and T. Greider. 1984. "Personal Well-Being in Rapid Growth and Stable Communities." *Rural Sociology* 49 (4): 541–52.

Kummerow, M., D. Moyer, and H. C. Jordahl Jr. 1981. "The Impact of Public Ownership on Private Lands in Polk and Burnett Counties, Wisconsin." Occasional
Paper no. 5. Madison: University of Wisconsin System, Cooperative Extension.

Ladd, C. E. 1999. *The Ladd Report.* New York: Free Press.

Landis, P. (1931) 1997. *Three Iron Mining Towns: A Study in Cultural Change.* Middleton, WI: Social Ecology Press.

Lane, M. 2002. "Buying Back and Caring for Country: Institutional Arrangements
and Possibilities for Indigenous Lands Management in Australia." *Society and Natural Resources* 15 (9): 827–46.

Lauber, T. B., M. L. Anthony, and B. A. Knuth. 2001. "Gender and Ethical Judg-
ments about Suburban Deer Management." *Society and Natural Resources* 14 (7):
571–84.

Lewis, P. 1995. "The Urban Invasion of Rural America: The Emergence of the
Galactic City." In *The Changing American Countryside,* edited by Emery E. Castle,
39–62. Lawrence: University Press of Kansas.

Liu, J. C., and T. Var. 1986. "Resident Attitudes toward Tourism Impacts in
Hawaii." *Annals of Tourism Research* 13 (2): 193–214.

Luedeke, M. 1995. "Considerations for Barrens Restoration in Burnett County." In
The Future of the Pine Barrens in Northwest Wisconsin: A Workshop Summary,
edited by Elizabeth A. Borgerding, Gerald A. Bartelt and Wendy M. McCown,
n.p. Proceedings of a workshop held at Solon Springs, WI, September 21–23,
1993. Madison: Wisconsin Department of Natural Resources.

Lund, F. P. 1975. *Iron River: My Home Town.* North St. Paul, MN: Lund.

Machlis, G. E., J. E. Force, and R. G. Balice. 1990. "Timber, Minerals, and Social
Change: An Exploratory Test of Two Resource-Dependent Communities." *Rural
Sociology* 55 (3): 411–24.

Maher, W. G., T. H. Townsend, and E. Dwight Sanderson. 1934. "A Study of Rural
Community Development in Waterville, New York." Cornell Agricultural Experiment Station Bulletin 608. Ithaca, NY: Cornell University.

Marans, R. W., and J. D. Wellman. 1978. *The Quality of Nonmetropolitan Living:
Evaluations, Behaviors, and Expectations of Northern Michigan Residents.* Ann
Arbor: Survey Research Center, Institute for Social Research, University of
Michigan.

Marchak, M. P. 1983. *Green Gold: The Forest Industry in British Columbia.* Vancou-
ver: University of British Columbia Press.

Marcouiller, D. W., G. P. Green, S. C. Deller, N. R. Sumathi, and D. L. Erkkila.
1996. *Recreational Homes and Regional Development.* Report no. G3651. Madison:
University of Wisconsin–Extension.

Marple, E. M. 1979. *The Hayward Lakes Region: A Century of History for the Visitor.*
Hayward, WI: Book Store.

Marsh, J., and K. Griffiths. 2006. "Cottage Country Landscapes: The Case of the
Kawartha Lakes Region, Ontario." In McIntyre, Williams, and McHugh, *Multiple Dwelling and Tourism,* 219–34.

Matarrita-Cascante, David, and A. E. Luloff. 2008. "Profiling Participative Residents in Western Communities." *Rural Sociology* 73 (1): 44–61.

Mather, A. S. 2001. "Forests of Consumption: Postproductivism, Postmaterialism, and the Postindustrial Forest." *Environment and Planning C: Government and Policy* 19 (2): 249–68.

McCool, S. F., and S. R. Martin. 1994. "Community Attachment and Attitudes towards Tourism Development." *Journal of Travel Research* 32 (3): 29–34.

McGranahan, D. 1999. *Natural Amenities Drive Rural Population Change.* Agricultural Economic Report no. 781. Washington, DC: U.S. Department of Agriculture.

McHugh, K. E. 2007. "Generational Consciousness and Retirement Communities." *Population, Space, and Place* 13 (4): 293–306.

McIntyre, N. 2006. Introduction to McIntyre, Williams, and McHugh, *Multiple Dwelling and Tourism*, 3–14.

McIntyre, N., and K. Pavlovich. 2006. "Changing Places: Amenity Coastal Communities in Transition." In McIntyre, Williams, and McHugh, *Multiple Dwelling and Tourism*, 239–61.

McIntyre, N., D. R. Williams, and K. E. McHugh, eds. 2006a. *Multiple Dwelling and Tourism: Negotiating Place, Home and Identity.* Cambridge, MA: CABI.

———. 2006b. "Multiple Dwellings: Prospect and Retrospect." In McIntyre, Williams, and McHugh, *Multiple Dwelling and Tourism*, 313–22.

Murphy, R. E. 1931. "The Geography of the Northwestern Pine Barrens of Wisconsin." *Transactions of the Wisconsin Academy of Science, Arts and Letters* 26: 96–120.

Nelson, A. C. 1992. "Characterizing Exurbia." *Journal of Planning Literature* 6 (4): 350–68.

Nelson, A. C., and K. J. Dueker. 1990. "The Exurbanization of America and Its Planning Policy Implications." *Journal of Planning Education and Research* 9 (2): 91–100.

Nelson, L. 1955. *Rural Sociology.* 2nd ed. New York: American Book.

Nelson, P. B. 2001. "Rural Restructuring in the American West: Land Use, Family and Class Discussions." *Journal of Rural Studies* 17 (4): 395–407.

———. 2002. "Perceptions of Restructuring in the Rural West." *Society and Natural Resources* 15 (10): 903–22.

Northwest Regional Planning Commission (NWRPC). 2000. *Northwest Sands Landscape Level Management Plan.* Pub-SS-953 2001. Madison: Wisconsin Department of Natural Resources.

———. 2008. "About NWRPC." Retrieved from http://www.nwrpc.com/about/.

Oliver, J. E. 2001. *Democracy in Suburbia.* Princeton, NJ: Princeton University Press.

Pahl, R. E. 1966. "The Rural-Urban Continuum." *Sociologia Ruralis* 6 (3–4): 299–329.

Peluso, N. L., C. R. Humphrey, and L. P. Fortmann. 1994. "The Rock, the Beach, and the Tidal Pool: People and Poverty in Natural Resource–Dependent Areas." *Society and Natural Resources* 7 (1): 23–38.

Periainen, K. 2006. "The Summer Cottage: A Dream in the Finnish Forest." In McIntyre, Williams, and McHugh, *Multiple Dwelling and Tourism*, 103–13. Cambridge, MA: CABI.

Perkins, H. C., and D. C. Thorns. 2006. "Home Away from Home: The Primary/Second-Home Relationship." In McIntyre, Williams, and McHugh, *Multiple Dwelling and Tourism*, 67–82. Cambridge, MA: CABI.

Pettingill, J. (1890) 1992. Personal correspondence. In *Iron River, Wisconsin Centennial, 1892–1992*, 63–76. Iron River, WI: Book Committee.

Pizam, A. 1978. "Spring Tourism's Impacts: The Social Cost to the Destination Community as Perceived by Its Residents." *Journal of Travel Research* 16 (4): 8–12.

Private Seasonal Housing in Wisconsin. 1966. Madison: Wisconsin Department of Resource Development.

Putnam, R. D. 2000. *Bowling Alone: The Collapse and Revival of American Community*. New York: Simon and Schuster.

Radeloff, V. C., D. J. Mladenoff, K. L. Manies., and M. S. Boyce. 1998. "Analyzing Forest Landscape Restoration Potential: Pre-settlement and Current Distribution of Oak in the Northwest Wisconsin Pine Barrens." *Transactions of the Wisconsin Academy of Sciences, Arts and Letters* 86:189–205.

Ragatz, R. L. 1970. "Vacation Homes in the Northeastern United States: Seasonality in Population Distribution." *Annals of American Association of Geographers* 60 (3): 447–55.

———. 1977. "Vacation Homes in Rural Areas: Towards a Model for Predicting Their Distribution and Occupancy Patterns." In Coppock 1977b, 181–94.

Ravenstein, E. 1876. "The Birthplace of the People and the Laws of Migration." *Geographical Magazine* 3:173–77, 201–6, 229–33.

Rengert, K. M, and R. E. Lang. 2001. "Cowboys and Cappuccino: The Emerging Diversity of the Rural West." Fannie Mae Foundation Census Note no. 4. Washington, DC: Fannie Mae Foundation.

Robertson, R. W. 1977. "Second Home Decisions: The Australian Context." In Coppock 1977b, 85–102.

Rohe, R. 1984. "The Myth of the Wild Wolf: Logging and River Improvement on a Wisconsin River." *Great Lakes Review* 10 (2): 24–35.

Romeril, M. 1984. "Coastal Tourism—The Experience of Great Britain." *Industry and Environment* 7 (1): 4–7

Rudzitis, G. 1999. "Amenities Increasingly Draw People to the Rural West." *Rural Development Perspectives* 14 (2): 9–13.

Salamon, S. 2003. *Newcomers to Old Towns: Suburbanization of the Heartland*. Chicago: University of Chicago Press.

Salazar, D. J., C. H. Schallau, and R. G. Lee. 1986. "The Growing Importance of Retirement Income in Timber-Dependent Areas." Research Paper PNW-359. U.S. Department of Agriculture, Forest Service Pacific Northwest Research Station, Portland, OR.

Sampson, R. J. 1988. "Local Friendship Ties and Community Attachment in Mass Society: A Multilevel Systemic Model." *American Sociological Review* 53 (5): 766–79.

Samra, G. H. El 1984. "Health and Tourism." *Industry and Environment* 7 (1): 7–11.

Sandercock, L. 1998. *Towards Cosmopolis: Planning for Multicultural Cities.* London: John Wiley.

Savage, C. (1934) 1992. Personal correspondence. In *Iron River, Wisconsin Centennial, 1892–1992,* 16–18. Iron River, WI: Book Committee.

Schnaiberg, J., J. Riera, M. G. Turner, and P. R. Voss. 2002. "Explaining Human Settlement Patterns in a Recreational Lake District: Vilas County, Wisconsin, USA." *Environmental Management* 30 (1): 24–34.

Schroeder, H. 2002. "Experiencing Nature in Special Places: Surveys in the North-Central Region." *Journal of Forestry* 100 (5): 8–14.

Schwarzweller, H. K. 1979. "Migration and the Changing Rural Scene." *Rural Sociology* 44 (1): 7–23.

Selwood, J., and M. Tonts. 2006. "Seeking Serenity: Homes Away from Home in Western Australia." In McIntyre, Williams, and McHugh, *Multiple Dwelling and Tourism,* 161–79. Cambridge, MA: CABI.

Sheldon, P. J., and T. Var. 1984. "Resident Attitudes to Tourism in North Wales." *Tourism Management* 5 (1): 40–47.

Shellito, B. A. 2006. "Second Home Distributions in the USA's Upper Great Lakes States: Analysis and Implications." In McIntyre, Williams, and McHugh, *Multiple Dwelling and Tourism,* 194–218. Cambridge, MA: CABI.

Shumway, J. M., and J. Lethbridge. 1998. "The Economic and Demographic Restructuring of Nonmetropolitan Counties in the Mountain West." In *Focus on Migration,* edited by Harry K. Schwarzweller and Brendan P. Mullan, 75–136. Research in Rural Sociology and Development 7. Stamford, CT: JAI Press.

Shumway, J. M., and S. M. Otterstrom 2001. "Spatial Patterns of Migration and Income Change in the Mountain West: The Dominance of Service-Based, Amenity-Rich Counties." *Professional Geographer* 53 (4): 492–502.

Smith, M. D., and R. S. Krannich. 1998. "Views toward Public Land Management Agencies: Are There Differences between Newcomers and Longer-Term Residents?" Paper presented at the Seventh Annual Symposium on Society and Resource Management, Columbia, MO, May 27–31.

———. 2000. "'Culture Clash' Revisited: Newcomer and Longer-Term Residents' Attitudes toward Land Use, Development, and Environmental Issues in Rural Communities of the Rocky Mountain West." *Rural Sociology* 65 (3): 396–421.

Smith, M. D., R. S. Krannich, and L. M. Hunter. 2001. "Growth, Decline, Stability, and Disruption: A Longitudinal Analysis of Social Well-Being in Four Western Rural Communities." *Rural Sociology* 66 (3): 425–50.

Smith, T. W. 1995. "Trends in Non-response Rates." *International Journal of Public Opinion Research* 7 (2): 157–71.

Smutny, G. 2002. "Patterns of Growth and Change: Depicting the Impacts of Restructuring in Idaho." *Professional Geographer* 54 (3): 438–53.

Sofranko, A. J., and F. C. Fliegel. 1980. "Rural Growth and Urban Newcomers." *Journal of Community Development Society* 11 (2): 53–68.

Spain, D. 1993. "Been-Heres versus Come-Heres: Negotiating Conflicting Community Identities." *Journal of the American Planning Association* 59 (2): 156–71.

State Comprehensive Outdoor Recreation Plan (SCORP). 2005. Madison: Wisconsin Department of Natural Resources.

Stedman, R. C. 2000. "Up North: A Social Psychology of Place." PhD diss., University of Wisconsin–Madison.

———. 2002. "Whose Community? Year Round and Seasonal Resident Differences in Place Attachment." Paper presented at the 65th Annual Meeting of the Rural Sociological Society, Chicago, August 14–18.

———. 2003. "Is It *Really* Just a Social Construction? The Contribution of the Physical Environment to Sense of Place." *Society and Natural Resources* 16 (8): 671–85.

———. 2006. "Places of Escape: Second-Home Meanings in Northern Wisconsin, USA." In McIntyre, Williams, and McHugh, *Multiple Dwelling and Tourism: Negotiating Place, Home and Identity,* edited by Norman McIntyre, Daniel R. Williams, and Kevin E. McHugh, 129–44. Cambridge, MA: CABI.

———. 2008. "What Do We 'Mean' by Place Meanings? Implications of Place Meanings for Managers and Practitioners." In *Understanding Concepts of Place in Recreation Research and Management,* edited by L. E. Kruger, T. E. Hall, and M. C. Stiefel, 109–34. Portland, OR: U.S. Department of Agriculture, Forest Service, Pacific Northwest Research Station.

Stedman, R. C., and R. Hammer. 2006. "Environmental Perception in a Rapidly Growing, Amenity-Rich Region: The Effects of Lakeshore Development on Perceived Water Quality in Vilas County, Wisconsin." *Society and Natural Resources* 19 (2): 137–51.

Steeh, C. G. 1981. "Trends in Nonresponse Rates, 1952–1979." *Public Opinion Quarterly* 45 (1): 40–57.

Stewart, S. I., and D. J. Stynes. 2006. "Second-Homes in the Upper Midwest." In McIntyre, Williams, and McHugh, *Multiple Dwelling and Tourism,* 180–93. Cambridge, MA: CABI.

Stinchcombe, A. L., C. Jones, and P. Sheatsley. 1981. "Nonresponse Bias for Attitude Questions." *Public Opinion Quarterly* 45 (3): 359–75.

Stonebraker, E. W. 2003. "How Smart Is Smart Growth in Wisconsin? A Preimplementation Evaluation of Locally Developed Comprehensive Land Use Plans." Master's thesis, University of Wisconsin–Madison.

Stroud, H. B. 1983. "Environmental Problems Associated with Large Recreational Subdivisions." *Professional Geographer* 35 (3): 303–13.

Stynes, D. J., and D. F. Holecek. 1982. "Michigan Great Lakes Recreational Boating: A Synthesis of Current Information." Michigan Sea Grant Technical Report MICHUSG82-204. Ann Arbor, MI: Michigan Sea Grant Program.

Swanson, L. E. 2001. "Rural Policy and Direct Local Participation: Democracy, Inclusiveness, Collective Agency, and Locality-Based Policy." *Rural Sociology* 66 (1): 1–21.

Taylor, J. E. 2004. "The Many Lives of the New West." *Western Historical Quarterly* 35 (2): 141–65.

Town of Sand Lake Comprehensive Plan. 2009. Town of Sand Lake, Burnett County, WI. Prepared by Foth Planning and Consulting. Retrieved from http://www.tn.sandlake.wi.gov/docs_by_cat_type.asp?doccatid=378&locid=163.

Tuan, Y. F. 1977. *Space and Place: The Perspective of Experience.* Minneapolis: University of Minnesota Press.

Turner, V., and E. Turner. 1982. "Religious Celebrations." In *Celebration: A World of Art and Ritual,* edited by V. W. Turner, 75–96. Washington, DC: Smithsonian Institution Press.

U.S. Census Bureau. 1900. Decennial Census. Vol. 1: Population: Population of States and Territories. Retrieved from http://www.census.gov/prod/www/abs/decennial/1900.htm.

———. 1970. *Compendium of the Nineteenth Census, Part 1—Population.* Washington, DC: U.S. Census Bureau.

———. 1980. *Compendium of the Twentieth Census, Part 1—Population.* Washington, DC: U. S. Census Bureau.

———. 1985. American Housing Survey. Published Reports H-151-85-1. Washington, DC: U. S. Census Bureau.

———. 1990. Decennial Census. American Fact Finder. Summary Files 1 and 3. Washington, DC: U. S. Census Bureau.

———. 1997. American Housing Survey. Published Reports H150/97. Washington, DC: U. S. Census Bureau.

———. 1999. County-to-County Worker Flow Files, Census 1990, Population Division, Journey-to-Work and Migration Statistics Branch. Created: November 5, 1999. Last revised: May 03, 2002. Retrieved June 24, 2003, from http://www.census.gov/population/www/socdemo/jtw_workerflow.html.

———. 2000a. Decennial Census. American Fact Finder. Summary File 1. http://factfinder.census.gov/servlet/DatasetMainPageServlet.

———. 2000b. Decennial Census. American Fact Finder. Summary File 3. http://factfinder.census.gov/servlet/DatasetMainPageServlet.

———. 2000c. Decennial Census. County to County Migration Files.

———. 2000d. Decennial Census. Geographic Definitions. http://www.census.gov/geo/www/geo_defn.html.

———. 2001a. "General Housing Characteristics: 2000, Census 2000 Summary File 1, Matrices H3, H4, H5, H6, H7, and H16." Retrieved February 2, 2002, from http://factfinder.census.gov/bf/_lang=en_vt_name=DEC_2000_SF1_U_QTH1_geo_id=01000US.html.

———. 2001b. State and County Quick Facts: 1990–2000. Published 03 July 2001. Washington, DC: U. S. Census Bureau.

———. 2002. Historical census of housing tables: Vacation homes. Retrieved February 3, 2003, from http://www.census.gov/hhes/www/housing/census/historic/vacation.html.

———. 2003a. American Housing Survey. Published Reports H150/03. Washington, DC: U. S. Census Bureau.

———. 2003b. County-to-County Worker Flow Files, Census 2000, Population Division, Journey-to-Work and Migration Statistics Branch. Created: March 6, 2003. Last revised: March 06, 2003, at 07:56:17 AM. Retrieved June 24, 2003, from http://www.census.gov/population/www/cen2000/commuting.html.

———. 2005. U.S. County Business Patterns. Retrieved from http://www.census.gov/econ/cbp/.

———. 2007. QWI Local Employment Data: Wisconsin. Retrieved from http://lehd.did.census.gov/led/datatools/qwiapp.html.

U.S. Department of Agriculture (USDA). Economic Research Service. 1997. "Understanding Rural America: County Types: Retirement-Destination Counties." Retrieved from http://www.ers.usda.gov/publications/aib710/aib710j.htm.

Vaske, J. J., M. P. Donnelly, D. R. Williams, and S. Jonker. 2001. "Demographic Influences on Environmental Value Orientations and Normative Beliefs about National Forest Management." *Society and Natural Resources* 14 (9): 761–76.

Verba, S., K. Schlozman, and H. Brady. 1995. *Voice and Equality.* Cambridge, MA: Harvard University Press.

Visser, G. 2004. "Second Homes and Local Development: Issues Arising from Cape Town's De Waterkant." *GeoJournal* 60 (3): 259–71.

Vogeler, I. 1986. *Wisconsin: A Geography.* With contributions by Harold Mayer, Brady Foust, and Richard Palm and with editorial assistance by Sharon Knopp. Boulder, CO: Westview Press.

Voss, P. R. 1980. "A Test of the 'Gangplank Syndrome' among Recent Migrants to the Upper Great Lakes Region." *Journal of the Community Development Society* 11 (1): 95–111.

Voss, P. R., and G. V. Fuguitt. 1979. "Turnaround Migration in the Upper Great Lakes Region." Population series no. 70–12. Madison: Applied Population Laboratory, Department of Rural Sociology, University of Wisconsin–Extension.

Walker, P., and L. Fortmann. 2003. "Whose Landscape? A Political Ecology of the 'Exurban' Sierra." *Cultural Geographies* 10 (4): 469–91.

Wilkinson, K. 1979. "Social Well-Being and Community." *Journal of the Community Development Society* 10 (1): 5–16.

———. 1991. *The Community in Rural America.* Middleton, WI: Social Ecology Press.

Williams, D. R., and S. R. Van Patten. 2006. "Home and Away? Creating Identities and Sustaining Places in a Multi-Centered World." In McIntyre, Williams, and McHugh, *Multiple Dwelling and Tourism*, 32–50.

Winkler, R., D. R. Field, A. E. Luloff, R. S. Krannich, and T. Williams. 2007. "Social Landscapes of the Inter-Mountain West: A Comparison of 'Old West' and 'New West' Communities." *Rural Sociology* 72 (3): 478–501.

Winton, W. 1980. "Agnes Kennedy." In *Historical Collections of Washburn County and the Surrounding Indianhead Country*, edited by E. Ward Winton and Kay Brown Winton, 233. Shell Lake, WI: Washburn County Historical Society.

Wisconsin Department of Natural Resources (DNR). 1996. *Northern Wisconsin's Lakes and Shorelands: A Report Examining a Resource under Pressure*. Madison: Wisconsin Department of Natural Resources.

———. 2000. *Northern Initiatives Lakes and Shorelands: Mid-Term Report Card, 1996–2000*. Madison: Wisconsin Department of Natural Resources.

Wisconsin's Comprehensive Planning Legislation. 1999. *Chapter 66.* General Municipality Law (s. 66.1001. Wis. Stats.).

Wisconsin Seasonal Residents Association. 2008. Homepage. Retrieved from http://wisra.org.

Wolfe, R. I. 1977. "Summer Cottages in Ontario: Purpose-Built for an Inessential Purpose." In Coppock 1977b, 17–34.

Wondolleck, J. M., and S. L. Yaffee. 2000. *Making Collaboration Work: Lessons from Innovation in Natural Resource Management*. Washington, DC: Island Press.

Yaffee, S. L. 1999. "Three Faces of Ecosystem Management." *Conservation Biology* 13(4): 713–25.

Yoffe, S. E. 2000. *Holiday Communities on Rangitoto Island, New Zealand*. Research in Anthropology and Linguistics 4. Auckland, NZ: University of Auckland.

Index

Tables are indicated by "t" following a page number.